A Practical Introduction to Sarbanes-Oxley (SOX)

Compliance:

Updated 2018

Jon Dye

DISCLAIMER AND IMPORTANT NOTE

The purpose of this book is to provide an overview and introduction to the basic requirements of the Sarbanes-Oxley (SOX) legislation. It also sets out the steps that corporations and corporations must take to comply with the legislation and gives a number of practical tips for individuals who are tasked with designing and operating SOX compliance frameworks. It is not however a comprehensive guide to SOX and, whilst the author reasonably believes the information provided to be correct (as at October 2016), the author accepts no liability for any defects or issues arising from any failures to comply with SOX legislation arising from using the information provided in this book. It is important that appropriate advice and counsel is taken by appropriately qualified professionals prior to embarking on a program of SOX compliance. The requirements and standards to be followed are updated continuously and should always be checked against the appropriate body's (PCAOB and SEC) website to ensure that the most up-to-date standards and requirements are followed.

ABOUT THE AUTHOR

Jon has been an accountant for 25 years, working in the fields of risk, controls and assurance. Jon worked initially for over 10 years with PwC, the international accountancy firm. Subsequently, he was the Head of SOX compliance for a UK bank, where he was responsible for designing, implementing and running a SOX compliance framework. More recently, Jon has been the CFO and Officer of a number of not-for-profit organizations and also provides training on SOX compliance issues for clients. He is currently Head of Assurance for Heriot-Watt University in the UK.

CONTENTS

Feedback and dedication   I

1   Introduction   1

2   Background   4

3   Summary of SOX legislation   11

4   Management certifications required by SOX   23

5   SOX objectives, materiality and internal controls   29

6   Developing and operating a SOX 404 compliance framework   45

7   IT internal controls   70

8   Outsourced processes and controls   87

9   Management certification frameworks   91

10   Other reforms introduced by SOX   96

11   Whistleblowing   101

12   Update February 2018   104

13   Reference materials   106

DEDICATION

My thanks must go to Norma Dye and Calum Galbraith for their support and encouragement to make this book a reality.

1 INTRODUCTION

It has been nearly 16 years since the Sarbanes-Oxley (SOX) Act was passed on 30 July 2002. When it was signed into law by President George W. Bush, it was against a backdrop of corporate scandal and public outrage. The prevailing laws and checks and balances in the system, which were meant to prevent corrupt corporate executives from carrying out fraud and misleading investors, or at the very least, if not prevent it, then make it public, had failed.

There were a number of corporate scandals which occurred around that time, but as we will see, it was the Enron scandal in particular, which unfolded during 2001, which was the main catalyst for action to be taken to strengthen the corporate governance code, introduce further steps to ensure that financial reporting by corporations was accurate, and to stiffen the penalties for executives and corporations who transgress.

The SOX legislation was hurried through the legislative process in a rare act of bipartisan support, with the result that the legislation was somewhat unclear and covers the same ground in different parts of the bill and sometimes in inconsistent ways. Some of the solutions to the problems identified had not been worked out at the point of the bill being passed, with the result that the Act gave powers to several bodies to enact solutions at a later date with the force of law.

Following the passing of the Act in 2002, the relevant standards and codes have evolved in response to pressure from various stakeholders in the process to further strengthen some areas and to give greater flexibility in others.

This book gives the reader an overview and summary of the backdrop and scandals leading up to the passing of the SOX Act and a summary of the main provisions of the Act itself. It also provides an overview of the main attestations required under SOX and then describes the main components of a management testing framework which is required to underpin those attestations. Finally, it gives a summary of some of the other main provisions in the Act designed to strengthen investor confidence in corporate financial reporting including: strengthening external auditor independence, establishing the independence of Audit Committees, strengthening the requirement for corporations to report significant corporate events to the market in real-time; and introducing safeguards for whistleblowers.

It should be mentioned in passing that there have been other significant changes to the US corporate governance framework since the SOX Act was passed, most notably with the passing of the Dodd-Frank Wall Street Reform and Consumer Protection Act (commonly referred to as the Dodd-Frank Act) in 2010. The Act was brought in to enact sweeping changes to the financial regulatory system in response to the financial crisis in 2008 and had the stated aim... "to promote the financial stability of the United States by improving accountability and transparency in the financial system, to end "too big to fail", to protect the American taxpayer by ending bailouts, to protect consumers from abusive financial services practices, and for other purposes." It reformed the regulatory landscape by creating important new government agencies, whilst disbanding and merging others. Existing agencies were given new powers and requirements to report periodically to Congress. New agencies created including the Financial Stability Oversight Council, the Office of Financial

Research, and the Bureau of Consumer Financial Protection.

The Dodd-Frank Act is outside the scope of this book although it updated the SOX provisions for whistleblowing which are referenced later.

President Trump has stated his intention to repeal the Dodd-Frank Act, and in June 2017 Congress voted to replace Dodd-Frank with the Financial CHOICE Act. This Act would roll back significant elements of the Dodd-Frank Act. It should be noted that at time of writing (February 2018), the Financial CHOICE Act had not passed the Senate (and therefore was not US law), and was considered unlikely to do so in its current form, given the current makeup of the Senate.

If Dodd-Frank is repealed, either completely or even in part, it will be interesting to see if there is a similar drive to reform SOX regulation, as equivalent arguments about cost and burdensome regulation versus investor and market protection apply similarly to SOX as for Dodd-Frank.

2 BACKGROUND

This chapter looks at the corporate legislation prior to the introduction of SOX and the corporate scandals which were the drivers for the introduction of the SOX legislation. Finally it goes on to look at the aims of the SOX legislation and the extent to which those aims may, or may not, have been achieved.

2.1 THE SECURITIES ACT 1933 AND THE SECURITIES EXCHANGE ACT 1934

Prior to the passing of the SOX Act, there were two pieces of legislation which were the main regulatory protection mechanisms for investors in relation to publicly listed corporations: The Securities Act 1933 and the follow up Securities Exchange Act 1934. These were passed by FDR during the Great Depression in order to improve investor confidence when investing in publicly listed corporations. Prior to this, investments were unregulated and the public was often duped into investing into worthless corporations with little or no protection.

The Securities Act 1933 set out the requirement for corporations to provide adequate, thorough and accurate financial information about securities being offered for sale to the public.

The Act introduced a detailed registration process which corporations must comply with when they offer securities for sale to the public in the form of a prospectus.

The Act requires accurate information to be made available to the public, however it does not prevent the public from being able to invest in bad ideas if it wishes – as one federal judge said, under the Act, investors are free to buy into any "hair-brained investment scheme" as long as it is accurately described.

The 1933 Act was silent on who enforced the law and it was quickly realized that a body was required to oversee regulatory corporate compliance. The Securities Exchange Act 1934 was passed the following year to rectify this gap. This Act created the Securities Exchange Commission (SEC) and gave it the power to develop its own rules which would have the force of federal law.

The SEC's purpose is to protect investors, maintain the integrity of the market, and to facilitate capital raising by corporations. It requires public corporations to make significant financial information accessible to the public in order for them to be aware of all factors surrounding an investment prior to buying into it. The aim is to provide a more efficient, active and transparent capital market, to improve and maintain the economy.

The SEC oversees key stakeholders in the market such as securities exchanges, securities brokers and deals, investment advisors and mutual funds as well as listed corporations themselves.

Every year, the SEC raises enforcement actions against those who violate securities laws including: insider trading, accounting fraud, or providing false or misleading information.

The 1933 and 1934 Acts are still in force and are still relevant today – however they have been enhanced and in some cases superseded by the SOX Act.

The SEC is responsible for overseeing compliance by public corporations with the SOX Act.

If this regime had been operating correctly then there would have been no need for the SOX Act to be passed in the first place but clearly it was not. We will take a brief look at what went wrong and what the SOX Act's objectives are to address the issues identified.

2.2 CORPORATE SCANDALS

There were a number of major corporate scandals which occurred in the early 2000s, many of which had similar recurring themes:

- Schemes such as off-balance sheet vehicles designed to hide expenses and liabilities from the company's financial statements.
- Annual reports and financial statements were produced which were misleading and gave investors an incorrect, and fraudulently optimistic, view of the company's finances and future.
- Powerful executives were running these corporations who, in some cases, were driven to misreport finances to drive up the company's share price to enable them to retain their jobs and receive inflated bonuses and compensation.
- External auditors who were perceived to be not sufficiently independent of Management, and were too ready and willing to sign-off financial statements which were at best questionable, and at worst fraudulently misleading, in the hope they would stay on the good side of senior management and continue to be able to sell lucrative non-audit services to their client.
- Boards, Audit Committees and Directors who were not sufficiently empowered to scrutinize and challenge powerful executives.
- Executives and others sold out shareholdings when the share price was artificially high without the market being aware of it.
- Whistleblowers were discouraged from coming forward and when they did – their warnings were not heeded.

- Documents were destroyed by management and auditors to prevent investigators from being able to examine financial records and management decisions.

There were a number of scandals in this period: Enron, WorldCom, Global Crossing, Tyco and Adelphia all happened at this time and many bore the same hallmarks. However, it was Enron scandal in particular that was the major catalyst for the development of the SOX legislation, which was at the time, the largest corporate bankruptcy in the history of the United States (and remains the third largest to this day).

2.3 ENRON

This section only gives a short overview of the Enron scandal and there are some excellent books and articles available which give more background to, and explanation of, the events and timeline of the Enron scandal.

Enron was an energy, commodities and services company based in Houston Texas which was created out of a merger between Houston Natural Gas and InterNorth – both regional players in the gas and energy market.

Enron grew rapidly after its foundation and by 2000, it employed over 20,000 staff and had reported annual revenues of more than $110 billion. This appeared to be one of the largest corporations in the US and, as at August 23 2000, the Enron share price reached a peak of $90 per share. By late 2001, Enron filed for bankruptcy in New York and by January 2002, Enron shares were worthless.

What had gone wrong? Enron was discovered to have grossly inflated its reported revenues and profits principally by hiding its liabilities and losses in 'Special Purposes Vehicles' (SPVs). These SPVs had complex and arcane accounting transactions between them and Enron. This meant Enron could hide its loss making activities and liabilities in the SPVs thus inflating the reported value of profits and asset's artificially in Enron's accounts.

A number of key Enron executives were found guilty of various counts of conspiracy, money laundering and fraud and served prison sentences. Kenneth Lay, who was the founder of Enron, and its CEO at the time of its demise, was found guilty of conspiracy and fraud but died on holiday whilst awaiting his appeal. Because Lay died prior to his appeal being heard, the court technically declared him not guilty using a process known as 'abatement', much to the fury of investors who had lost money, who felt that justice had not been served.

Enron's external auditor had been Arthur Andersen, which was at the time, by some measures, the largest accountancy and professional services firm in the world. It was also embroiled in the scandal and in June 2002 was convicted for obstruction of justice in relation to the Enron scandal due to the shredding of a large number of documents related to its audit of Enron. Arthur Andersen was also involved in a number of other corporate scandals e.g. it was also the external auditor of WorldCom (which collapsed on 25 July 2002 and was an even bigger corporate bankruptcy than Enron).

In 2002, Arthur Andersen, a firm which had reported annual revenues of $9.3 billion and employed 85,000 people worldwide, closed down, with many of the partners and staff transferring to other offices of international accounting firms.

It should be noted that the Supreme Court, in 31 May 2005, set aside Arthur Andersen's conviction due to defects in the original court case. However, this judgement came far too late for Arthur Andersen which was in effect out of business, with its reputation ruined, by this point.

In light of the Enron scandal, and other significant corporate scandals, there was widespread public outrage that major corporations, which had the outward appearance of integrity and reliability, could produce financial statements which were so manifestly untrue and misleading, causing investors large and small to lose their money. In addition, the fact that these financial statements were audited and signed off by a major accounting firm, which many investors took as a sign of trust that they were reliable, turned out to be worthless and contributed to investors overall lack of trust in the market. This situation meant that there was a major political driver to address this problem - and address it quickly.

The SOX Act was drafted and passed in a very short space of time in a rare act of bipartisan support, with remarkably little dissent in the political process.

The Bill was sponsored by Paul Sarbanes, a Democratic congressman, in Congress and passed, with only three members voting against. Michael Oxley, a Republican senator, sponsored the Bill in the Senate where it passed 99-0.

The Act was signed into law by President George W. Bush on 30 July 2002. The WorldCom corporation had filed for bankruptcy on 25 July, only five days prior to the SOX Act being signed. WorldCom was an even bigger bankruptcy that Enron, which was at the time the biggest corporate collapse in US history. (Today Lehman Bros is the biggest corporate collapse in US history, with WorldCom second, and Enron third).

It is worth pointing out that many of the acts committed at Enron, and elsewhere in other major corporate scandals at the time, were already illegal under existing law, however there was a feeling that 'something must be done'.

There were four main objectives in the SOX legislation to attempt to address the underlying causes of the corporate scandals:

- Hold Management more accountable for the actions of the company – particularly in relation to financial reporting.
- Improve company disclosures to the market over significant events and transactions – sometimes in real-time.
- Improve the independence and accountability of external audit firms so that the integrity of external audit firms' opinions and audit reports could be restored and investors could have confidence in them.
- Improve the SEC's ability to oversee the market and hold corporations accountable by reviewing their disclosures.

The SOX Act was published in something of a rush, and so it was not particularly well drafted in parts. Parts of the legislation overlaps with other parts – sometimes reiterating points, sometimes appearing to contradict. In other parts of the legislation, it authorizes the SEC and the newly created Public Company Accounting Oversight Board (PCAOB), which was set up by the SOX Act, to carry out research and initiate solutions (which would then carry the force of law), as the solutions to some of the identified problems were not known at the time the legislation was drafted, and legislators did not want to wait.

Since the SOX Act has been published, in nearly 15 years, the SEC, PCAOB and the courts have clarified parts of the legislation, and the requirements for compliance, so there is a much more clearly understood compliance framework to be followed. The following chapters set out a summary of the Act and the key steps which must be followed to comply with it.

3 SUMMARY OF SOX LEGISLATION

This chapter provides an overview and summary of the SOX legislation and has been summarized by each section – or Title – of the Act.

3.1 TITLE I – REFORM OF THE AUDIT PROFESSION

The purpose of this section of the Act was to introduce better oversight and regulation of the audit profession. Prior to the SOX Act, the audit profession was self-regulated by the American Institute of Certified Public Accountants (AICPA). The lack of a rigorous independent audit was seen by many as a key factor in the major corporate scandals and collapses which were the drivers behind the legislation. This section of the Act created the Public Company Accounting Oversight Board (PCAOB). The role of the PCAOB is to independently oversee the audit profession and ensure that auditors are independent, perform their work to professional standards, to monitor and inspect audit firms, and take out sanctions against firms whose work does not meet standards set or transgress rules in other ways.

The PCAOB has seven statutory duties under SOX 101(c):

- Register external audit firms that prepare audit reports;

- Establish "auditing, quality control, ethics, independence" and other standards relating to preparation of audit reports;
- Conduct inspections of external audit firms on a regular basis;
- Conduct investigations, hold disciplinary proceedings, and impose appropriate sanctions on external audit firms which break the laws, professional standards and quality thresholds;
- Enforce compliance with the SOX Act, rules of the PCAOB, professional standards, and securities laws;
- Set the annual budget for the PCAOB and manage operations of the PCAOB and its staff; and
- Perform other duties and functions as appropriate.

Its main responsibilities are to register all audit firms who can carry out audits, and carry out regular inspections of firms to ensure that registered firms conduct audits to the relevant quality and standards. All firms are inspected at least once every three years, and larger firms are inspected annually. The PCAOB can also enforce disciplinary measures against audit firms which do not meet the required standards including: required improvements to audit processes, fines and disbarment.

TIP: The PCAOB also has taken over the development and publication of applicable audit standards which are freely available on the PCAOB's website: www.pcaobus.org. These standards are updated on a regular basis, so it makes sense to check back periodically to check for updates. Updates are usually highlighted at the start of the standard in the form of a press release highlighting the change. Whilst these standards are written from the perspective of the external auditor, Management should perform its work to underpin the attestations required under SOX to the same standard as the external auditor (in relation to the assessment of internal controls), so these standards should be used in relation to Management's SOX compliance work also.

This section of the Act also required firms carrying out audits to have a second review partner who must review and provide a concurrent sign-off to the signing partner. This is thought to provide an additional layer of independence for external audit firms which, prior to this point, only required one partner to sign-off financial statements.

This section of the Act also requires auditors to retain all working papers (electronic and paper) which provide evidence of the audit work performed and support the audit conclusions reached for a minimum of 7 years. Samples of work papers are reviewed by the PCAOB during the inspections of firms to verify the audit conclusions reached.

The SOX Act also requires audit firms to carry out an evaluation of the internal control environment over financial reporting and report the conclusion of that work alongside the opinion on the financial statements which they previously had to provide. This is covered in more detail in chapter 6 – Developing and operating a SOX 404 compliance framework. This part of the Act also requires auditors to describe any material weaknesses found in the internal control framework and document any material non-compliance with standards.

3.2 TITLE II – AUDITOR INDEPENDENCE

This section of the SOX Act enforces the requirements for auditors to be independent of corporations that they audit. Lack of independence of audit firms was seen as a factor in some of the corporate scandals. In particular, the amount of non-audit advisory work which some audit firms carried out at their clients was perceived to have impaired external audit firms' ability to form independent judgement of their client's financial statements.

Almost all services, except for the external audit itself, are banned under SOX from being carried out by a company's external auditor.

The following is a list of the types of non-audit services which were typically carried out by external auditors and are now banned (note that the list is not exhaustive):

- Bookkeeping
- IT services
- Valuation of assets
- Actuarial services
- Internal audit outsourcing
- Management functions
- Human resources or headhunting
- Investment banking / Investment broking
- Legal services
- Expert services (e.g. regulatory compliance)

TIP: Virtually all non-audit services are banned from being carried out by the company's external auditor. One notable exception to the list of non-audit services which can be carried out by the external auditor is tax services, which are generally allowed. All non-audit services which are to be carried out by the external auditor must be explicitly approved by the company's Audit Committee. All fees earned by the external auditor must be disclosed in the company's financial statements. All audit and non-audit fees must be disclosed separately.

This section of the Act also requires the external auditor to report to the Audit Committee on the accounting policies used in the audit.

To further address previous concerns raised about auditor independence, the lead audit partner (and the new role of reviewing partner created under SOX legislation) cannot carry out that role for more than five years before they must rotate off.

In addition, if a senior executive has been recruited from the external auditor, then the external auditor faces a one-year ban if the executive was employed in the one year period preceding the start of the audit.

3.3   TITLE III – BUILDING CORPORATE ACCOUNTABILITY

This section of the Act has a number of elements – all of which are designed to improve the corporate accountability of a company's Management. The first part covers the requirement for a company to establish an Audit Committee. (The detailed requirements are covered in chapter 10 – Other reforms introduced by SOX.)

It also requires the CEO and CFO to make a number of certifications over the financial statements, some of which were new under SOX:

- SEC filings do not have untrue statements or material omissions.
- Financial statements, in all material respects, fairly represent the financial situation and operational results.
- The CEO and CFO are responsible for internal controls, and that internal controls are designed to ensure management receives all material information.
- Internal controls have been reviewed within 90 days prior to the annual report date.
- Whether there were any significant changes made to the internal controls in the period.

This goes to the heart of the SOX compliance process and is covered off in much more detail within Chapter 6 – Developing and operating a SOX 404 compliance process.

This section of the Act also makes it unlawful for corporate personnel to exert 'improper influence' on an audit which might result in materially misleading financial statements. (This was almost certainly illegal under existing legislation, but the SOX Act made this type of action explicitly unlawful).

It also requires the CEO and CFO to forfeit bonuses and certain compensation which must be paid to the company if there is a requirement for the company to issue re-statements of prior period financial statements (normally re-statements are only made if a material error or misstatement is found at a later date in an earlier set of financial statements).

This section of the Act bans Directors and Executives from trading shares during blackout periods around period ends. It also obliges corporate lawyers appearing before SEC to report violation of securities laws and breaches of fiduciary duty.

The Act allows the SEC to set up and maintain a fund paid for by fines collected under violations of the SOX and securities Acts, which is used for the benefit of victims of securities law violations.

3.4 TITLE IV – OFF-BALANCE SHEET TRANSACTIONS, ADJUSTMENTS, LOANS AND CODES OF ETHICS

This section of the SOX Act covers a number of required disclosures, bans loans from corporations to executives and deals with ethics codes.

This section requires the disclosure of all material corrections made to the financial statements during the course of the external audit. Prior to this, external auditors could require corporations to make material corrections to their financial statements (or external auditors could qualify or refuse to sign audit reports) but the users of financial statements would not be aware that this had happened.

> **TIP:** Draft final financial statements, which are provided to external auditors at the start of the annual audit process, should be in as final a state as possible to reduce the risk that the external auditor (or Management) finds a material misstatement during the external audit process which would then need to be disclosed as a material adjustment to the draft accounts. Corporations who disclose that

material misstatements were found, and had to be adjusted for, during the external audit process are likely to be viewed negatively by the SEC, investors, markets and other stakeholders. In-progress draft financial statements may be given to external auditors earlier in the year-end process by Management to be helpful and assist external auditors in their planning. However Management should make it clear that any in-progress drafts are still subject to change, and are not the declared 'final draft' from which both Management and external auditor will work from (and report material changes if they were required) to sign-off the financial statements.

Material off-balance sheet transactions and relationships, which had been such a feature of the corporate scandals of the early 2000's, are now also required to be disclosed (given that the whole purpose of off-balance sheet transactions and relationships is to conceal expenses and liabilities – the requirement to disclose them here is presumably a deterrent to using them in the first place!)

This section prohibits corporations from making loans to its executives.

It also requires disclosure to the market, within two working days, of changes to shareholdings by a company's executives.

This section contains the famous section 404 which requires corporations to include a report on their internal controls for the first time. This report requires Management (the CEO and CFO) to say that it is responsible for the internal control structure and procedures for financial reporting. The report must also include management's assessment of the effectiveness of internal controls for the previous year and include the external auditor's assessment on internal controls also. This area is covered in much more detail in chapter 6 – Developing and operating a SOX 404 compliance framework.

Under this section of the Act, corporations must disclose whether they have adopted a code of ethics for their senior financial employees and whether their audit committee has at least one financial expert.

This section of the Act also requires the SEC to conduct regular reviews of disclosure documents which corporations file with the SEC to ensure compliance with regulations.

3.5   TITLE V – IMPROVING AND PROTECTING ANALYST INTEGRITY

Another area where it was felt that improvements were required by the SOX Act to address issues in some of the corporate failures was in the integrity and independence of the analyst community. Analysts work for large corporate banks and ratings agencies, follow publicly listed corporations and regularly publish research which is used by investors to make investment decisions. It was felt that some analysts did not carry out their role in the market effectively in the run up to some of the major corporate scandals. Analysts did not necessarily call out concerns and issues with some of these corporations prior to their collapse at least in part due to perceived conflict of interest issues, and possibly being 'leant on' by the management of corporations themselves not to publish negative research reports.

In this section of the Act, there are a number of provisions which are all designed to strengthen the integrity and independence of the analyst community.

One of the key areas of perceived conflict of interest was that a number of analysts work for divisions of investment banks whose other role is to sell corporate finance services to major listed corporations and so therefore might have a vested interest in suppressing negative reports about potential or actual clients.

The SOX Act restricts the capacity of investment bankers to pre-approve research reports written by analysts, and requires that analysts are not line managed by investment bankers. It also prohibits employers from retaliating against analysts who write negative research reports into specific corporations. It also requires analysts who have any potential conflict of interests to make public disclosures about those conflicts of interests, so that the investing public can factor this into the potential weight they would place on any analyst research and investment recommendations made by analysts.

3.6 TITLE VI – SPENDING AUTHORITY

This section of the Act authorizes the SEC to spend more than $98m in the set up and hiring of staff for the PCAOB. It also gives the SEC authority to censure individuals for unethical or improper conduct. It also requires the SEC to take into account any orders made by individual state security commissions in relation to limiting activities and operations of brokers and dealers.

3.7 TITLE VII – RESEARCH AND STUDIES

The SOX Act was written in something of a rush in response to the corporate scandals and so, in some cases, there were a number of problems which had been identified but not necessarily the solutions. In these cases, the SOX Act funded research into the perceived problems and then report back at a later date with proposed solutions that could be adopted by the SEC, with the effect of law.

The research that this section of the Act funded included:

- The consolidation of public accounting firms and its impact on the markets.
- The role of credit rating agencies and their impact on the market.
- The role investment banks and financial advisors played into the manipulation of financial reports and transactions.

3.8 TITLE VIII – CRIMINAL FRAUD AND WHISTLEBLOWER PROTECTION

This section of the Act imposes criminal penalties, to a maximum 10 years in prison, for knowingly destroying, altering, concealing, or falsifying records with the intent to obstruct or influence a federal investigation or bankruptcy. (This was of course illegal in any event prior to SOX but the Act does re-iterate the fact those specific activities are fraudulent and illegal and increases the penalties).

There are also sanctions for external audit and Management who fail to maintain all audit or SOX 404 compliance testing work papers for a minimum of seven years.

This section of the Act also makes certain debts in relation to fines and sanctions for violation of securities laws non-dischargeable in bankruptcy. In other words, fines cannot be written off by external auditors and company executives by going down the route of bankruptcy.

It also increases the statute of limitations for investors who may want to sue corporations, audit firms and individuals for securities fraud violations. Investors can sue no later than two years after the discovery of the violation or five years after the date of the violation itself.

There are also penalties for executives who target whistleblowers by imposing fines and imprisonment of up to 25 years. (More information on whistleblowers can be found at Chapter 10 - Other reforms introduced by SOX).

3.9 TITLE IX – PENALTIES FOR CRIME

This section imposes and increases the amounts in relation to fines and prison time that executives and external auditors can expect if they commit crimes under SOX and securities acts. It increases the penalties for mail and wire fraud from five to 20 years in prison. It also establishes criminal liability for non-compliance under the certification rules for financial statements established under Title III.

It establishes a maximum of 20 years in prison for executives who deliberately submit a non- compliant certification. Crucially it also establishes that there is now criminal liability for executives who submit a non-compliant certification but did so unwittingly (i.e. even if they did so negligently but in good faith). In this case there is still a potential penalty for up to 10 years in prison.

3.10 TITLE X – CORPORATE TAX RETURNS

This section of the Act states that federal income tax returns should be signed off by the company's CEO.

3.11 TITLE XI – PRISON TERMS, BLACKLISTS AND PAYMENT FREEZES

This section of the Act updates the law to impose a 20 year maximum prison term for impeding an official investigation or tampering with a record. It also allows the SEC to obtain a temporary injunction to freeze any 'extraordinary payments' to Management or employees who may be under investigation for possible violation of securities law. There was no definition in the Act as to what constitutes an 'extraordinary payment' however there have been some litigation and other government definitions which have been put in place since then.

It also prohibits executives who have been found guilty of violations of state or federal securities laws from serving as officers or directors of publicly traded corporations.

It also updates the penalties for crimes committed against the Securities Exchange Act 1934 to a maximum fine of $25m and up to 20 years in prison.

3.12 SCOPE OF THE SOX ACT

The SOX Act applies to all publicly listed corporations – that is corporations who are listed on an exchange (e.g. NYSE, NASDAQ). Section 207 of the SOX Act also identifies other corporations which are in-scope for SOX including:

- Corporations with more than 500 investors and $10m in assets;
- Corporations with more than 300 investors;
- Voluntary filers; and
- Corporations with registrations pending.

So the SOX act applies to all but the smallest corporations. In addition there are several provisions within the Act which also apply to all corporations:

- The requirement to keep records for seven years;
- The protections for employee whistleblowers; and
- Criminal provisions for those who commit fraud and conspiracy.

4 MANAGEMENT CERTIFICATIONS REQUIRED BY SOX

One of the main areas where SOX strengthened management accountability was in respect of the management certifications which must now accompany financial statements. These are specified in s302, s404 and s906 of the SOX Act which cover the requirements and scope of the certifications and the penalties for getting them wrong. These sections of the Act overlap with each other and can even be seen to be inconsistent, which is the result of the legislation being drafted in a rush.

Who is management? The SOX Act makes it clear that the certifications must be signed by both the Chief Executive Officer (CEO) and Chief Financial Officer (CFO). These two individuals are now responsible, both in civil and criminal terms, for the certifications they must sign under SOX, and the Act makes it clear that they cannot avoid or devolve responsibility for that to anyone else.

Under s302 of SOX, the CEO and CFO must certify the "appropriateness of the financial statements and disclosures contained in the periodic report, and that those financial statements and disclosures fairly present, in all material respects, the operations and financial condition of the issuer". This applies to the Annual

Report submitted annually in the 10-K filing to the SEC and applies to any amendments subsequently filed to the 10-K. It also to the 10-Q quarterly financial reports filed with the SEC. Refer to Chapter 10 – Other reforms introduced by SOX, for more information on filings by corporations with the SEC.

The SOX legislation was written very precisely (at this point!) to ensure that there could be no backsliding from management by caveating or qualifying the certifications which the CEO and CFO must make.

4.1   s302 PARAGRAPH 1: REVIEW OF FINANCIAL STATEMENTS

The CEO and CFO must certify they have reviewed the report they are certifying. Presumably this was to stop CEOs and CFOs from saying that they were unaware of errors or misstatements in the financial statements because they had not reviewed them. Now the CEO and CFO must say they have reviewed the report.

4.2   s302 PARAGRAPH 2: MATERIAL ACCURACY

The CEO and CFO must state that, based on their knowledge, the report does not contain any material misstatements (in the numeric data), or materially misleading statements (in the accompanying text).

4.3   s302 PARAGRAPH 3: FAIR REPRESENTATION OF FINANCIAL DATA

The CEO and CFO must state that, based on their knowledge, the financial information contained in the financial statements fairly presents, in all material respects, the company's financial condition, results of operations, and cash flow for the periods being reported.

The SEC has since issued clarification that this includes (but not limited to): footnotes, financial data in the annual report, discussion and analysis of the financial information.

> **TIP:** It is not good enough just to have materially correct numbers. This section of the legislation requires the CEO and CFO to certify that the accompanying text is not materially misleading also. So, for example, if the figures say you the company has made a loss, and the text says it has had a great year trading – then it will fail this section.

4.4 s302 PARAGRAPH 4: DISCLOSURE CONTROLS AND PROCEDURES

This section overlaps with SOX s404 which is discussed in more depth later. It only applies to the annual report filed with the 10-K and not to the 10-Q quarterly financial statements. It says that the CEO and CFO are responsible for establishing and maintaining internal controls. It requires management (CEO and CFO) to ensure controls are adequate to ensure that material or significant information about the company comes to the attention of officers. (This section of the Act is designed to prevent the CEO and CFO from claiming that a material issue occurred at a lower level within the company, but that they were not aware of it, so they signed off the financial statements in ignorance.) This section makes it clear that the CEO and CFO are responsible in any event for designing controls such that all material or significant information about the company is escalated to them.

This section also requires Management (the CEO and CFO) to certify that they have evaluated the effectiveness of the company's internal controls as of a date within 90 days prior to the issuance of the annual report. Management must also take ownership of the conclusions reached about the evaluation of the effectiveness of the company's internal controls.

4.5 s302 PARAGRAPH 5: DISCLOSURES TO AUDIT COMMITTEE AND AUDITORS

Management must disclose the following to its Audit Committee and to its external auditors:

- All significant deficiencies (defined later) in the design or operation of internal controls which could adversely affect the company's ability to record, process, process, summarize, and report financial data and have identified for the company's external auditors any material weaknesses in internal controls.
- Any fraud, whether or not material, that involves Management or other employees who have a significant role in the company's internal controls.

The definitions of the terms used above are explained in more detail in chapter 5 – SOX objectives, materiality and internal controls.

4.6   s302 PARAGRAPH 6: CHANGES TO INTERNAL CONTROLS

Management must provide information about changes to internal controls. The CEO and CFO must certify that they have included in the annual report whether or not there were significant changes in internal controls or other factors that could significant affect internal controls subsequent to the date of their evaluation, including any corrective actions with regard to significant deficiencies and material weaknesses.

4.7   s404 INTERNAL CONTROL REPORT

The now famous (or infamous) section 404 of the SOX Act deals with the requirement to include an internal control report in the company's annual report.   (It also overlaps with requirements outlined in s302 above).

This requires management (CEO and CFO) to include an internal report in the company's annual report which includes the following points:

- It must state that it is the responsibility of management for establishing and maintaining an adequate internal control structure and procedures for financial reporting.
- It must contain an assessment by Management, as of the end of the company's most recent financial year, of the effectiveness of the internal control structure and company's procedures.

s404 also requires the external auditor to certify management's opinion on the internal control reports. The external auditor must ensure Management has:

• Accepted responsibility for the effectiveness of the company's internal control structures and financial reporting procedures.
• Evaluated the effectiveness of the company's internal control using suitable criteria.
• Supported the auditor's evaluation of internal controls with sufficient documentation.
• Presented a written assessment of the effectiveness of the company's internal control.

The certification and evaluation of internal controls by the CEO and CFO must be underpinned by an annual process for identifying and evaluating relevant internal controls – this is covered in much more detail in Chapter 6 – Developing and operating a SOX 404 compliance framework.

The SEC and the SOX Act requires that Management and the external auditors must evaluate the internal controls in place separately, and Management cannot delegate its responsibility for evaluating internal controls to the external auditors.

4.8 s.906 CRIMINAL PENALTIES

This section repeats, to some extent, the certification requirements already documented at s302 of the SOX legislation. However, it goes on to say that if the CEO or CFO deliberately submits a certification under SOX that they know to be false, then they face penalties of up to a maximum of 20 years in prison and a fine of $5m. It also goes on to say that if the CEO or CFO inadvertently submits a certification in good faith that they believe to be true but is found to be false, then this is still classed as a criminal offence with a maximum penalty of 10 years in prison and $1m fine.

5 SOX OBJECTIVES, MATERIALITY AND INTERNAL CONTROLS

Before we go further, it is important at this stage to develop an understanding of what we mean by SOX objectives, materiality and internal controls in relation to the management attestations required under SOX legislation. It is important to remember that these terms have wider definitions in business, and in this chapter we will look at them specifically in relation to their impact on SOX compliance and financial reporting.

5.1 SOX OBJECTIVES

We have already seen the management attestations required under SOX legislation. When Management is evaluating the company's internal controls over financial reporting, this translates into two objectives: the risk of material misstatement within the financial statements (often shortened to Material Misstatement Risk (MMR)); and the fraud risk.

Management's evaluation of internal controls would therefore focus on the effectiveness of the internal controls that mitigate the two risks above and provide appropriate assurance to Management.

5.2 MATERIALITY AND MATERIAL MISSTATEMENT

RISK

The words 'material' and 'materiality' are used a lot within the SOX legislation, in the SEC guidance and PCAOB standards.

> **TIP:** In the PCAOB's audit standards, used by external auditors to plan their audits of corporations, standard AS 2015: "Consideration of Materiality in Planning and Performing an Audit" contains the definition of materiality in use by the audit profession and Management should use the same definition to plan its work.

That standard notes that "In interpreting the federal securities laws, the Supreme Court of the United States has held that a fact is material if there is "a substantial likelihood that the . . . fact would have been viewed by the reasonable investor as having significantly altered the 'total mix' of information made available." As the Supreme Court has noted, determinations of materiality require "delicate assessments of the inferences a 'reasonable shareholder' would draw from a given set of facts and the significance of those inferences to him . . . ."

In other words, if you gave a "reasonable investor" a set of financial statements, an error or misstatement is material if it is large or significant enough that a reasonable investor might reach the wrong (or different) judgments and conclusions about the finances, operations and/or prospects for the company. If a company declares a profit of $1bn and there is a $1 error in that profit, then the error clearly is immaterial. In other words, even allowing for the error, an investor would form the same judgements and conclusions about a company that declares a profit of $999,999,999 as $1bn! Similarly if a company declares a profit of $1bn and there is a $2bn error such that the company has in reality made a loss of $1bn, then that is clearly a material error. An investor is clearly going to form the wrong investment conclusions about a company that declares a $1bn profit instead of a $1bn loss.

However, at the margins it is a judgment call as to the limit of the size of an error that would be defined as material. Accountants do like to come up with rations such as 5% of balance sheet or 10% of revenues in order to define a 'hard' number for materiality. However, it should be remembered that, depending on a particular company's size and circumstances, materiality can vary and significantly can in fact sometimes be quite small. (e.g. if a company has a declared a small profit, an error which would tip the company into declaring a loss might be seen as material to investor, but in reality might in fact be a small number).

Therefore what is material and by corollary, what is immaterial, is somewhat judgmental in terms of certifying a company's financial statements by Management for the purposes of compliance with SOX. But in broad terms, Management is saying that, even if there are errors in the financial statements, the errors are not large or significant enough either individually, or in combination, that a reasonable investor could review the financial statements and form the wrong judgments and conclusions about the company, its finances, operations and prospects.

TIP: It is not just numbers within financial statements that can be materially wrong. The text issued by Management accompanying financial statements can be materially wrong if reasonable investors form the wrong impressions and judgments about a company's performance by reading that text. If Management describes the company, in the annual report, as having had a great year, when it has made a loss, or says the company has exciting prospects for the future when it is about to run out of money, then these statements might also be reasonably described as being materially wrong or misleading!

5.3 INTERNAL CONTROLS

In the development and operation of a SOX 404 compliance framework, as we have seen, Management must have a framework of internal controls over financial reporting and must evaluate its effectiveness (and include that evaluation in its internal control report within the annual report).

It is therefore vitally important to develop a good understanding of what we mean by internal controls in the context of SOX objectives, material misstatement risk and fraud risk.

The SEC says that internal control (in the context of SOX 404 compliance) is a "process designed to provide reasonable assurance regarding the reliability of financial reporting and preparation of financial statements". The SEC says these should include policies and procedures that address:

- Good recordkeeping;
- Recording and authorisation of transactions; and
- Fraud detection.

5.4 COSO FRAMEWORK

The SOX legislation requires that Management bases its assessment of the effectiveness of a company's internal controls over financial reporting using a suitable set of standards established by recognized experts. It is silent on which framework must be used, however the SEC recognizes the framework established by the Committee of Sponsoring Organizations of the Treadway Commission (COSO) Internal Control – Integrated Framework as an acceptable framework to underpin the assessment performed by Management of its internal control framework over financial reporting.

TIP: Whilst there are other frameworks, the reality is that the COSO framework is the definitive standard which is recognized by the SEC, external audit firms, aligns with the PCAOB's Audit Standard AS 2201 and aligns with the major SOX software packages on the market also. It should also be remembered that, whilst the COSO framework is the standard framework used for SOX 404 compliance, the COSO Internal Control - Integrated Framework is a comprehensive framework to allow corporations to fully identify, evaluate and control the complete range of risks they might face, and therefore has a much wider scope than would be required to achieve SOX 404 compliance. Care should be taken to only focus on the relevant elements which are required to achieve SOX 404 objectives (material misstatement risk, fraud risk) otherwise compliance testing can stray into evaluating areas and controls which are not relevant for SOX 404 compliance purposes. More information on the COSO Internal Control – Integrated Framework can be found at: www.coso.org. The framework can be purchased at the COSO website – note that "COSO – Internal Control Integrated Framework" Executive Summary document is free and provides an excellent overview of the elements of the framework.

COSO defines internal control as "…a process, effected by an entity's board of directors, Management, and other personnel, designed to provide reasonable assurance regarding the achievement of objectives relating to operations, reporting and compliance."

The COSO framework splits into five components and 17 control objectives within them to allow Management to identify specific internal control objectives and activities. The five components, as defined by COSO, which contribute to a company's overall internal control framework are:

A) Control environment;
B) Risk assessment;
C) Control activities;
D) Information and communication; and

E) Monitoring activities.

COSO goes on to define 17 control objectives which sit within the five components. These control objectives should be used when identifying suitable controls to satisfy SOX compliance objectives, and every control identified should link to at least one of the 17 objectives.

A. Control environment

1. The organization demonstrates a commitment to integrity and ethical values.

2. The board of directors demonstrates independence from Management and exercises oversight of the development and performance of internal control.

3. Management establishes, with board oversight, structures, reporting lines, and appropriate authorities and responsibilities in the pursuit of objectives.

4. The organization demonstrates a commitment to attract, develop, and retain competent individuals in alignment with objectives.

5. The organization holds individuals accountable for their internal control responsibilities in the pursuit of objectives.

B. Risk assessment

6. The organization specifies objectives with sufficient clarity to enable the identification and assessment of risk relating to objectives.

7. The organization identifies risk to the achievement of its objectives across the entity and analyzes risks as a basis for determining how the risks should be managed.

8. The organization considers the potential for fraud in assessing risks to the achievement of objectives.

9. The organization identifies and assesses changes that could significantly affect the system of internal control.

C. Control activities

10. The organization selects and develops control activities that contribute to the mitigation of risks to the achievement of objectives to acceptable levels.

11. The organization selects and develops general control activities over technology to support the achievement of objectives.

12. The organization deploys control activities through policies that establish what is expected and procedures that put policies into action.

D. Information and communication

13. The organization obtains or generates and uses relevant, quality information to support the functioning of internal control.

14. The organization internally communicates information, including objectives and responsibilities for internal control, necessary to support the functioning of internal control.

15. The organization communicates with external parties regarding matters affecting the functioning of internal control.

E. Monitoring activities

16. The organization selects, develops, and performs ongoing and/or separate evaluations to ascertain whether the components of internal control are present and functioning.

17. The organization evaluates and communicates internal control

deficiencies in a timely manner to those parties responsible for taking corrective action, including senior management and the board of directors, as appropriate.

> **TIP:** When all suitable controls have been identified, it is worth grouping them against each of the 17 control objectives so that you can then review if sufficient controls have been identified to satisfy each of the 17 control objectives. If not, it may be that additional controls need to be identified or it may be that there is a gap in the control framework.

5.5 INTERNAL CONTROL DEFINITIONS

In simple terms, internal controls, in the context of SOX 404 compliance, are activities or processes which contribute to the prevention or detection of errors in financial transactions which might lead to material misstatements in financial reporting or to prevent or detect fraud. Controls might also be activities which support and/or monitor these controls being carried out effectively. From a SOX 404 compliance perspective, a control is effective if it reduces the likelihood to a 'remote' possibility that a material misstatement has made it through to the financial statements and reporting.

Entity-level controls

Some internal control activities are described as entity-level controls. These generally are activities whose effects are felt across the whole business rather than to an individual business process, or specific type of transaction. There are a number of different types of entity-level internal controls which can be categorized as follows:

- Controls related to the control environment;
- Controls over management override;
- Risk assessment processes operated by the company;

- Centralized processing and controls e.g. shared services;
- Controls which monitor results;
- Controls to monitor the effectiveness of other controls, including activities of assurance functions, internal audit, the Audit Committee, and any self-assessment programs running over risks, issues and/or controls;
- Controls over the period-end financial reporting process; and
- Policies that address significant business control and risk management practices.

Business process level / transaction level internal controls

On the other hand corporations will also have specific internal controls which operate within individual business processes, and are designed to prevent or detect errors relating to one or more specific account assertions (these are discussed in more detail in Chapter 6: section 6.2 Planning) in the transaction processing at each stage in the business process (or may prevent or detect fraud within the business process). These are commonly known as business process level controls or transaction level internal controls. Examples of business process level preventative and detective internal controls are as follows:

Preventative and detective internal controls

Preventative controls: This type of control prevents financial errors or fraud from happening prior to it occurring.

Examples of this type of business process controls are:

System validation controls: Often validation rules are built into systems which prevent certain errors from being input into financial records (or other fields). These might include validation such as: fields which cannot be input blank; numeric fields; fields which must be within certain financial tolerances (such as tax fields); journal entries which must balance; and suppliers which must match previously input details.

Authorization controls: Controls requiring the prior authorization of expense claims, or invoices prior to being input into the financial systems, for example, would be preventative controls.

Detective controls: This type of control detects financial errors and/or fraud which have already taken place. The effectiveness of these controls lie in the adequacy of the challenge and follow up process which takes place over questionable transactions and ultimately the extent to which errors and/or fraud is followed up, detected and corrected in an appropriate timeframe. (If errors in transactions are allowed to remain uncorrected at the year-end then a control might reasonably be considered to be ineffective). Examples of detective controls are:

Reconciliation controls: Reconciliations are carried out between two (or sometimes more) different sources of financial data to identify discrepancies which should then be followed up and corrected. The most well-known type of reconciliation is the bank reconciliation which reconciles the bank account(s) of a company with its financial systems. On the basis that most financial transactions of a company will also go through its bank account(s) (both in terms of income and expenditure), a bank reconciliation that reconciles the transactions and balances in the bank statements with the company's financial records on a regular basis is a good overall confirmation of the accuracy of the financial systems and records which a company holds. Like all detective controls, reconciliations are only effective when discrepancies are followed up and errors are corrected in a timely manner.

Review and monitoring controls: Review controls will typically involve the review of financial reports or transactions which might involve review for unusual items, discrepancies, errors and/or fraud. As previously described, review or monitoring controls are only effective if errors or fraud are followed up and corrected in an appropriate timeframe. There should also be appropriate segregation of duties between those employees performing the process and those conducting the review or monitoring processes.

Automated and manual controls

Controls can either be automated or manual in their operation.

Automated controls are built into financial or IT systems themselves e.g. validation or access controls. They are therefore reliant on the IT application functioning as expected and so reliant on IT general controls operating over the IT systems and environment. This is covered in much more detail in chapter 7 – IT internal controls. However, in theory, if automated controls are designed and implemented sufficiently, they will work 100% of the time and so are considered to be very effective.

Manual controls on the other hand are reliant on one or more employees carrying out the control. Therefore an assessment of the effectiveness of the control over a period of time would include considerations such as: do the employees have the skills, training and experience to carry out the control effectively; are they authorized to carry out the control; is the control performed in a timely manner; what arrangements are in place to ensure the control is still carried out when employees who normally carry out the control are on holiday, or absent through sickness. Manual controls normally involve some degree of judgement by the employee and are therefore often are more inconsistent in their level of effectiveness.

> **TIP:** For manual controls, in order to facilitate SOX compliance, control ownership should be assigned to a single owner who should be clear about their responsibilities with respect to the control (and should understand the requirements for SOX compliance and consequences if not carried out correctly). Control owners should understand the actions required to carry out the control to a satisfactory standard and the escalation required if there is an issue

with the effectiveness of the control. Control owners should also have the accountability for their control(s) documented within their role description. Role evaluation processes for the control owner should include an evaluation of the discharge of their responsibilities with respect to the control. It may be more appropriate for the control owner to be the manager responsible for the control rather than the employee who carries it out, but this will depend on the relative seniority of the employees involved. There should be appropriate segregation of duties between employees carrying out processes and control owners to ensure that controls cannot be circumvented or control documentation altered.

Control documentation

Control documentation (this may include paper and electronic records) should be maintained by Management and employees for at least 7 years. In general terms, sufficient documentation should be maintained to allow a different employee with the same level of skill, experience and training to perform the same control and get the same or similar conclusions. For detective controls, the documentation retained should include evidence of follow up of discrepancies and potential errors, and evidence of any corrections made to the financial records, when and by whom. All control documentation should clearly identify who performed the control and when, including all follow up and corrective actions taken, and if the controls has been subject to independent management review or oversight (which they should be) then this should also be documented and when it was performed. On a very practical level, whilst it is good practice to get employees to sign control documentation as evidence that the control was performed by them, some signatures are illegible and it is important that the documentation also clearly states who performed the control, and also the reviewer, if relevant. This is the evidence will be tested to support Management's SOX s302 and s404 compliance attestations. It will also be tested to support the external auditor's work and opinion.

TIP: If control documentation is incomplete or absent then generally the control should be treated as if it had not operated effectively for the period where the evidence documentation is incomplete or absent.

5.6 INTERNAL CONTROL DEFICIENCIES

In the context of SOX s404 compliance objectives, a control is said to be deficient when the design or operation of a control does not allow managers or employees to prevent or detect and correct financial errors, misstatements or fraud in a timely manner.

Design deficiency: A control is said to be deficient in its design either because: a control is missing completely from the business process and therefore allows errors to pass into the financial systems and ultimately financial statements uncorrected and/or allows fraud to occur and remain undetected; or a control has been implemented, however it has not been designed properly and does not achieve the desired control objective, even if it appears to be operating as intended.

Operational deficiency: A control is said to be operationally deficient if a control has not been performed correctly and in the case of a manual control, this may be because the employee performing the control does not have authority, skills, training or experience to perform the control effectively.

5.7 REMEDIATION OF DEFICIENT INTERNAL CONTROLS

If a control deficiency is identified then the potential impact on the SOX s404 compliance framework and financial statements must be considered and that is covered in Chapter 6 – Developing and operating a SOX 404 compliance framework: section 6.4 Testing conclusions and reporting.

However, in any event suitable remediation of the control deficiency should be agreed with line management. The nature of the remediation involved will depend on the type of deficiency identified and may include:

Design deficiency: Design and implementation of one or more new additional control(s) to supplement the existing controls in place; or redesign of existing controls to meet the control objectives.

Operational deficiency: Management action to rectify operational deficiencies in the control effectiveness. This may include management oversight processes to ensure the control has been carried out, and/or that potential issues have been followed up and corrections carried out on a timely basis; it may require changing the control owner to an employee with the appropriate skills and experience, or provision of additional training for employees carrying out the control.

Line management owns the business processes and controls operating within them and therefore line management must also own the remediation actions to rectify issues identified. All actions agreed should be owned by a suitably senior member of management and the seniority will depend on the severity of the issue and the complexity and scale of the actions required to fix it. Given the importance of rectifying the issue(s) identified both for SOX s404 compliance and attestation purposes but also for the appropriate running and operation of the business, the owner of the actions to fix the issue(s) should be held accountable for ensuring the agreed actions are carried out. This may include making them aware of possible sanctions and/or disciplinary action which might be applied if agreed actions are ignored or not implemented in time.

> **TIP:** Management should agree and own the remediation actions to be taken to rectify the control deficiency. Many corporations have frameworks for recording control issues and remediation actions (e.g. those raised by internal audit) and if possible, SOX 404 internal control issues and remediation actions should be recorded and monitored using the same framework. There may be other parties who have a stake in the implementation of a successful fix to the control deficiency e.g. the external auditor, internal audit, other assurance functions such as risk management or regulatory compliance, other business line management; and it is therefore important to involve all relevant stakeholders when agreeing the rectification of a control deficiency. The rectification may fix the control from a SOX s404 compliance perspective (i.e. preventing or detecting financial errors and misstatements and/or fraud), however it may not achieve wider business goals which may also be required, such as meeting customer requirements or regulatory requirements. It is important that rectification requirements and actions are agreed by all stakeholders who are relevant.

> **TIP:** The actions agreed with Management to rectify the deficiency should follow the standard 'SMART' acronym to ensure that they are precise and will achieve the desired outcome:
>
> *Specific* – Actions to be taken should be clear and specific so there is no room for ambiguity after the event as to what was expected.
>
> *Measurable* – All actions should be measurable, such that Management and SOX compliance testing can verify that the agreed actions have taken place, and that the expected outcomes were achieved.
>
> *Acceptable* – The agreed actions must be accepted by all parties as achieving the required outcome of rectifying the deficiency.

Realistic – All actions must be realistic and have a reasonable prospect of being carried out in the timescale.

Timely – There should be an agreed timeline for the actions to be taken to rectify the control deficiency and this will be a factor in the overall assessment of the impact of the control deficiency both in the context of the overall attestations that Management must make in relation to internal controls, but also in the broader context of the controlled running of the business.

TIP: Some actions to rectify control deficiencies may be complex or significant, and therefore may require a longer timeframe to develop and implement. In these cases, Management may have to consider putting in place other compensating, or interim controls, which provide a level of assurance while the actions are being carried out.

When Management has confirmed that it has carried out the agreed actions, it may be appropriate to carry out testing to confirm that the actions are in place and the control is now working effectively. The results of this testing would normally be included in reporting to senior management and potentially the Audit Committee. If the actions to rectify the issue have not been taken, or are found to be ineffective, and the control is still not effective, this would be escalated to an appropriate level of senior management and/or the Audit Committee for further action to be taken.

6 DEVELOPING AND OPERATING A SOX 404 COMPLIANCE FRAMEWORK

As we have seen previously, Management (which under SOX is strictly defined as the CEO and CFO) must make attestations under s302 and s404 of the SOX legislation. In this section, we are going to look at the work that must be undertaken to underpin those conclusions and attestations.

There is an annual cycle of testing work which must be undertaken to support Management's attestations under SOX s404 in the annual report. SOX s404 says that the annual report must include an internal control report, certified by the CEO and CFO which says:

- It is the responsibility of Management for establishing and maintaining an adequate internal control structure and procedures for financial reporting.
- It must contain an assessment by Management, as of the end of the company's most recent financial year, of the effectiveness of the internal control structure and company's procedures.

Therefore Management must undertake a program of testing to support these attestations. The program of work must be designed to be sufficient to allow the CEO and CFO to sign off that appropriate internal controls are in place and are working adequately (or make the appropriate disclosures if they are not). At the same time, the program of work must be efficiently designed to only test the relevant controls and processes which contribute to the SOX 404 compliance attestations. All corporations will have numerous other controls which are relevant to running the business effectively and efficiently but will not be relevant for SOX 404 compliance testing, and so it is important that plans do not stray into testing irrelevant controls.

The SOX Act also requires the external auditor to review the internal controls over financial reporting as well as Management (this is in addition to the external auditor's function – which it had prior to SOX – of signing off on the material accuracy of the financial statements).

> **TIP:** Management and external audit must perform independent assessments of the internal controls over financial reporting and so it is important for Management's credibility that Management and the external auditors reach the same conclusions over the internal controls. It is important therefore, without compromising the external auditor's independence, to replicate as closely as possible the work of the external auditor to minimize the risk that both groups (Management and external auditor) reach different conclusions. In this regard, the external auditor must follow the requirements of the audit standard AS2201 – An Audit of Internal Control over Financial Reporting (previously called Audit Standard no. 5) , the text of which can be found at www.pcaobus.org. It makes sense therefore for Management to use the same standard to design and carry out its testing processes for SOX 404 compliance purposes.

6.1 SOX 404 ANNUAL COMPLIANCE CYCLE

The SOX 404 compliance annual cycle comprises the following elements which we shall look at in turn:

- Planning;
- Walkthrough;
- Detailed testing; and
- Assessment of deficiencies identified and overall conclusions.

> **TIP:** The PCAOB's audit standard AS2201 – 'An Audit of Internal Control Over Financial Reporting That Is Integrated with An Audit of Financial Statements' gives valuable information about how the SOX 404 compliance cycle and testing should be approached. Whilst it is written from the perspective of external auditors, it can be easily applied to the approach Management should take to compliance testing (bearing in mind an objective of Management should be to arrive at the same conclusions over internal control as the external auditor in any event).

6.2 SOX 404 PLANNING PROCESS

The planning process is carried out annually (and may be revisited during the year) to develop a program of testing. Successful planning should ensure that the program of internal control testing is appropriately designed to provide sufficient coverage and assurance to allow Management to make the appropriate disclosures and attestations under SOX. It also should ensure that the overall compliance process is as efficient as possible by eliminating accounts and testing which is superfluous to the overall SOX 404 management attestation conclusions.

This section looks at the steps in the planning process required to develop a program of testing work from first principles. This would generally only occur in practice if it is the first year of a company's compliance with SOX (which would not be the case for most corporations), or for example, if SOX was required for the first time over a new business unit or company which had been acquired.

In practice, the planning process, in an ongoing cycle of compliance, will involve focusing on assessment of changes to the business from prior years. This includes an assessment of changes to the risk profile and the required changes to the SOX compliance testing framework.

Top down approach

The audit standard AS2201 says that a top-down approach should be used to select the controls to test for SOX 404 compliance. A top-down approach begins at the financial statement level and with the understanding of the overall risks to internal control over financial reporting. The focus should first be on entity-level controls and then works down to significant accounts and disclosures, and their relevant assertions (these terms are explained later). This approach directs attention to accounts, disclosures, and assertions that present a reasonable possibility of material misstatement to the financial statements and related disclosures. The next step would be to build an understanding of the risks in the company's processes, and then select for testing those controls that sufficiently address the assessed risk of misstatement to each relevant assertion.

Step 1: Inputs to the planning process

There are a number of inputs to the planning process which should be considered to assess the risk profile of the organization and changes to it from prior years:

- Annual budgets and any year-to-date results which might exist;
- Prior year SOX 404 compliance planning documentation (if it exists);
- Existing documentation of internal controls over financial reporting;
- Matters affecting the industry in which the company operates;
- Matters relating to the company's business;

- The extent of any changes, if any, in the company, its operations, and impact on internal controls over financial reporting;
- Control deficiencies previously identified and the extent to which they have been addressed;
- Legal or regulatory matters (to the extent they may impact on SOX 404 attestations);
- Type and extent of available evidence relating to the effectiveness of internal control over financial reporting;
- Risk assessments from the business line or other assurance functions;
- Any fraud committed in prior year and the current fraud risk assessment; and
- Complexity of company's operations.

The above points all feed into the assessment of inherent risk and changes to the operations of the organisation, which may require changes or additions to focus of work performed from the prior year.

Step 2: Identification of entity-level internal controls over financial reporting

WE have already discussed entity-level controls and the COSO internal control framework in Chapter 5. At this stage, we should identify the key entity-level controls which support the integrity of financial reporting. Using the risk assessment performed above in step one and using the COSO framework (5 components and 17 control objectives), you should identify the key entity-level controls that provide assurance to Management over the integrity of financial reporting and disclosures. As we saw in Chapter 5, the entity-level controls should map to at least one of the 17 control objectives in the COSO framework. In practice, this would be done for the first year in discussion with Board members, Executives, senior managers and managers to understand the processes and controls in place. When you believe all key entity-level controls have been identified, they should be grouped under the 17 control objectives to assess if the controls identified provide sufficient assurance over each of the 17 objectives or whether there are any gaps. If there are any weaknesses or gaps, it is worth having further discussion with Management as there may be further entity-level controls in place that address the gaps which you have not yet identified. It may also be that there are in fact gaps and these should be treated as control deficiencies and the process should be followed for remediating deficient controls – outlined at Chapter 5: section 5.7 Remediation of deficient internal controls. The impact of the control deficiencies should be fed into the overall conclusions of testing described at Chapter 6: section 6 Testing conclusions and reporting. (If entity-level control gaps are remediated early enough in the financial year then there may be no impact overall on the control environment by the year end).

Step 3: Assessment of preliminary materiality

We have already looked at the definition of materiality at Chapter 5: section 5.2. A preliminary judgement of materiality should be made at this stage using the previous year's annual financial outturn and budgets set for the financial year (along with the previous assessment of materiality if it is available), along with the assessment of inherent business risk performed in step one.

TIP: Preliminary materiality which is set at this stage in the planning process should be revisited, both in the run up to the year end (using expected annual outturn results) and then at year end using draft full-year results. This is performed to verify the preliminary materiality set at the planning stage remains adequate. It may be necessary to revise materiality should the full-year results be significantly lower than budgets or expectations. This may, of course, require consequential changes or additions to the testing which was previously planned. (The sooner any additional testing required is identified, the easier it will be to be able to carry it out and factor in the results to the overall SOX 404 compliance conclusions prior to reporting deadlines.)

The next step in the planning process is to identify the significant accounts from the financial statements and trial balance.

> **TIP:** Significant accounts are those accounts which may require detailed testing to be performed on the internal controls over the transactions which feed into them and the balances. Conversely accounts which are not significant may be eliminated from detailed testing - on the grounds of risk and preliminary materiality. (However it should be noted that just because an account's projected year-end balance is below preliminary materiality this should not automatically rule out detailed testing from being carried out.) This is discussed in more detail below.

Step 4: Identification of significant accounts

Using the prior year financial statements (or draft financial statements for the current year if available), identify the source of each item of financial data in the financial statements. This will usually be either an individual trial balance account, or the total of a group of trial balance accounts. It should be remembered that whilst most of the items in the financial statements are derived from the trial balance, some numbers in the financial statements – particularly those in supporting notes - come from other sources and sub ledgers e.g. fixed asset register, which will bring these sub ledgers and processes around them in-scope for potential detailed testing.

The preliminary materiality should be applied at this stage to identify the trial balance accounts (or groups of accounts) which are likely to be significant and therefore in-scope for testing. If the prior year full-year outturn trial balance has been used, then an analytical review should be performed between the prior year actual outturn and current year budget to identify the changes from prior year.

Step 5: Identification of account assertions

Audit Standard 2201 defines 5 account assertions – a subset of which will apply to each trial balance account (or group of accounts) identified in Step 4, depending on the type of account it is. The following are the five account assertions defined in the audit standard and define the control objectives which will apply to the transactions which flow into the account (note it will only be a subset of the 5 that will apply to any particular account):

- Existence or Occurrence: This objective requires that only valid accurate transactions are posted into the account (applies to all trial balance accounts)
- Completeness: This objective requires that all valid transactions are posted to the account (applies to all trial balance accounts);
- Valuation or allocation: This object requires that appropriate valuation or allocation of transactions and balances has been applied using the appropriately qualified professional judgement. (applies to trial balance accounts where the balance or transactions have an element of judgmental valuation or allocation which may be based on professional opinion)
- Rights and obligations: This objective requires that the rights and obligations have been correctly recorded in the company's financial records (applies to trial balance accounts involved in the company's rights e.g. debtors and obligations e.g. creditors)

> **TIP:** It is worth considering the risk of fraud as a sixth account assertion alongside the five account assertions above.

The account assertions should be recorded against all significant accounts.

Step 6: Assessment of Material Misstatement Risk (MMR)

The Material Misstatement Risk (MMR) should be assessed for each of the significant accounts (or groups of accounts) identified. The MMR assesses the risk that there might be a material error or misstatement in those accounts. The MMR assessment will use the risk assessment carried out earlier in the planning process and should also link to at least one (or more) of the 17 COSO control objectives that we already have defined.

TIP: Should trial balance accounts be automatically defined as non-significant and therefore excluded from requirement for detailed testing because they have immaterial balances or nil balances?

No – the MMR risk might require that detailed testing is required even if the account balance is immaterial or nil. Here are two examples of MMR risk which might require detailed testing to be carried out over immaterial balances:

- An account balance might be immaterial because it is materially misstated due to an error (e.g. a cut-off error at period end) and therefore it ought to have a material balance. The number of transactions that flow through the account during the period might be a risk factor to consider even if the balance is small at year-end.
- During risk assessment, consideration should be given to the scenario that Management may have manipulated the balance to be materially misstated and therefore smaller than it should be (unfortunately you have to think the unthinkable during the SOX compliance process!) In terms of possible Management manipulation, the objectives might be maximization of profit and increasing net assets. This translates in to possible manipulation of the earnings and balance sheet as follows:
  - Revenues accounts – overstatement
  - Expense accounts – understatement
  - Asset accounts – overstatement
  - Liabilities – understatement

So it follows that expense and liabilities type accounts might be understated by Management and therefore, although balances may be immaterial or zero, there may be a risk (which should be evaluated) that they might be materially misstated and the controls (likely to be entity-level financial review controls and possibly business process level controls) which mitigate that risk should be brought into scope.

These factors and decision-making around those accounts should be considered and documented during the planning process when considering which accounts are in-scope (and out of scope) for walkthroughs and detailed testing.

Step 7: Determination of business cycles and the need for walkthroughs and detailed testing

The next step in the planning process is to identify the business processes or cycles that drive transactions into the significant accounts (or groups of accounts) in the trial balance/financial statements. In an ongoing SOX 404 planning cycle, this will have been done in prior years, but will require to be updated for any business changes and/or change to MMR since the prior year.

It should be noted that certain types of account will be driven by several business cycles e.g. cash will be driven by Accounts Payable but also by Accounts Receivable business cycles.

The business processes identified here will potentially require walkthrough (described later) to understand the individual steps in the business process, key IT systems used and the internal controls, which will require to be tested, which prevent or detect errors in the financial transactions that relate to the relevant account assertions.

For each significant account or groups of accounts, using the account assertions identified, MMR assessed and preliminary materiality, the level of walkthrough and likely extent of detailed testing required should be documented. (Walkthroughs and detailed testing are described in more detail in the following sections).

In some cases, business processing may be outsourced to a third-party service provider, the SOX 404 compliance requirements in those circumstances are described in Chapter 8 – Outsourced processes and controls. The planning process should document the steps to be taken to get the relevant assurance from service organizations.

Step 8: Period end reporting

The audit standard AS2201 defines the controls over the period end reporting process and the production of the financial statements as entity-level controls since they address financial reporting risk over the whole company. They should be documented as part of the planning process as a separate section of the planning document.

Period end reporting controls are considered to be entity-level internal controls however they are controls over the business processes which operate specifically at period ends in the production of the financial statements. These may include controls over the following:

- Procedures used to enter transaction totals into the general ledger;
- Procedures related to the selection and application of accounting policies;
- Procedures used to initiate, authorize, record, and process journal entries in the general ledger;
- Procedures used to record recurring and nonrecurring adjustments to the annual and quarterly financial statements; and
- Procedures for preparing annual and quarterly financial statements and related disclosures.

Step 9: Fraud risk planning

The assessment of fraud risk should be used to plan the identification and testing of internal controls which mitigate the risk of fraud both for entity-level controls and during the walkthroughs and business process level control identification and testing. As discussed earlier, the fraud risk assertion should be considered alongside the other financial misstatement risk assertions when identifying the entity-level controls and business process level controls to test.

When identifying internal controls to address fraud risk – the following types of controls and risks should be considered:

- Controls over significant transactions that are outside the normal course of business for the company or that otherwise appear to be unusual due to their timing, size, or nature;
- Controls over significant unusual transactions, particularly those that result in late or unusual journal entries;
- Controls over journal entries and adjustments made in the period-end financial reporting process;
- Controls over related party transactions;
- Controls related to significant management estimates; and
- Controls that mitigate incentives for, and pressures on, Management to falsify or inappropriately manage financial results.

Step 10: Planning for IT internal controls

During the planning process, it is useful to identify key IT systems within the business that are in-scope for financial reporting (these are normally understood and documented in more detail during walkthroughs). These would include the financial systems themselves, as well as other IT systems used in the key business process cycles identified during the planning process.

An assessment of the extent to which the SOX 404 compliance process relies on the correct processing by IT systems, and the performance of automated reporting and controls must be performed. This will then identify the extent to which work will require to be performed on IT internal controls. IT internal controls are described in more detail in chapter 7.

There are 3 types of IT internal control:

-   IT entity-level controls – these should be identified during the planning phase and should again relate to the COSO objectives.
-   IT application controls – these controls operate within individual business processes and would be identified during the walkthrough phase and tested as part of detailed testing.
-   IT general controls – these are the controls which underpin the correct operation of the in-scope IT systems and planning work is required to identify the relevant IT general controls which relate to the in-scope IT systems identified.

The planning process should document the approach to be taken to taken over the testing of key IT entity-level controls and IT general controls. IT application controls would be identified during the walkthrough phase.

Step 11: Documentation

The planning process is now complete and all of the steps and decisions taken above must be documented. It may also be useful for a SOX 404 compliance planning document to be produced. The SOX 404 compliance plan would normally document the key planning steps as follows:

- Assessment of inherent risk – Documentation of the assessment of inherent risk, focusing on changes to the business, risk profile from prior years and likely impact on the SOX 404 compliance testing program of work.

- Entity-level controls – Key entity-level controls which will require to be tested and the likely level of testing to be performed.

- Preliminary materiality – The materiality that has been set at the planning stage (noting that this will require to be re-evaluated at the year-end – and there may be consequential impacts on the in-scope significant accounts and/or the level of detailed testing which might require to be performed.)

- Significant accounts – The significant accounts, or groups of accounts, which have been identified as in-scope (and those which are non-significant and why that is the case). The account assertions and fraud risk should be identified against each of the significant accounts, or groups of accounts. The assessment of MMR should also be documented against each significant account, or groups of accounts. The business cycles or processes which drive transactions to the significant accounts or groups of accounts should be documented against each significant account and the likely level of walkthrough and detailed testing required should also be documented.

The plan would also document the timing of the work to be performed, the likely resource requirement and the reporting and outputs of the work.

TIP: It may also be useful to set out expectations in relation to the level of co-operation and input to the process which will be required by Management and business employees in the plan. It is also useful to use the plan to set expectations of key stakeholders such as: external audit, Audit Committee, CEO and CFO (after all this will drive their attestations) and other senior management. The plan is also useful to frame discussions with line management in relation to the practicalities of carrying out walkthroughs and detailed testing.

6.3 WALKTHROUGHS

As we have seen, the planning process will have identified a number of business process cycles which are material, or likely to be material, to significant accounts in the financial statements and disclosures. At this point, walkthroughs must be performed on each of the business processes. If walkthroughs have already been performed on the business processes in prior years, then the primary purpose of the walkthrough would be to update the information already stored on the business process and focus on any changes since the prior year. If it is a new business process, or year one of the SOX compliance process, then a walkthrough would be performed to build the knowledge of the business process, the IT systems used, and the key internal controls in place and document that.

Walkthroughs are carried out by taking a single transaction and following it from origination (i.e. the earliest point in the business process where the transaction is created in the first place) through all of the steps of the business process, identifying the key controls in place, until the transaction has reached the financial systems and ultimately the financial statements. The walkthrough also identifies all IT systems involved in the business process.

Walkthroughs should also consider whether there are appropriate segregation of duties between personnel carrying out processes and controls and those with review and oversight responsibilities. If there are inadequate segregation of duties, it may impair the effectiveness of controls in place to prevent errors and/or fraud. This is a particular issue for smaller organizations who may have small finance or accounting functions.

> **TIP:** The single transaction chosen to follow for the walkthrough must be representative of the full population of transactions handled by the business process. If the business process deals with a number of classes of transactions, sometimes following slightly different processing and controls, it may be more appropriate to select a

transaction from each class of transaction to follow through. For example a walkthrough of Accounts Payable will follow the raising of purchase orders, receipt of goods, invoices and ultimately payment. However, there will usually be a separate process for recording of credit notes and, if different to the overall Accounts Payable process, should be subject to its own walkthrough process.

The walkthrough of the business process can be performed using the following methods:

Inquiry – Discussions and interviews with the employees who operate the business process and key controls;

Observation – Observing the business processes and controls being carried out in real-time;

Inspection of relevant documentation – This could include relevant policies and procedural documentation for the business process; systems documentation; and control documentation.

Re-performance of controls – Controls can be re-performed to test their effectiveness. (This is done less often at walkthroughs and more often performed when detailed testing of the control is carried out.)

The output of the walkthrough is full documentation including a description of all of the steps in the business process with all IT systems involved; personnel and locations involved in processing; and all key controls identified which prevent or detect financial errors covering the relevant financial statement assertions identified during the planning process and risk of fraud.

The documentation can often include a flowchart which gives a pictorial representation of the key processing steps and the points where the key controls are carried out. All IT systems that are involved in the processing should be documented.

Control design deficiencies – Once the walkthrough has been completed and documented, the controls identified should be assessed to identify control design deficiencies in the business process. This may be because there is a control missing from the business process completely or there is a control which is not designed correctly to achieve the control objective.

> **TIP:** The most efficient way to consider if there are any control design deficiencies in the business process is to examine each step of the business process in turn. For each business process step, examine the financial statement assertions identified in planning (and risk of fraud), and consider how the internal controls identified prevent or detect financial errors from being introduced at that step in the process, or how those controls prevent or detect fraud. The internal controls identified should sufficiently mitigate the risk of financial errors in the accuracy of an individual transaction and in the completeness of processing of the population of financial transaction records at each step in the business process. Internal controls should also mitigate the risk of fraud being carried out undetected.

> **TIP:** Once any potential internal control gaps have been identified, it is useful to have a further conversation with the relevant employees who operate the business process as there are often other internal controls operating that you may not have been made aware of, which may address the control gaps identified at this point.

Note that the operational effectiveness of internal controls is not normally assessed at the walkthrough stage. Operational effectiveness is only assessed at the detailed testing stage.

6.4 DETAILED TESTING OF INTERNAL CONTROLS

Detailed testing must be carried out over the key internal controls identified to assess their operational effectiveness. Note that testing will include testing of key entity-level controls identified; key business process controls identified during walkthroughs (manual and automated); and IT entity-level general controls if required.

Testing should address whether the control is operating as designed (i.e. it is achieving the control objective) and if it is a manual control, whether the employee carrying out the control has the authority and competence to carry out the control. The Audit Standard AS2201 gives the external auditor (and therefore Management) significant discretion in the way that detailed testing is carried out.

Interim testing is carried out on a sample basis to test the operational effectiveness of the control between the start of the financial period in question and the testing date. The later that interim testing is carried out during the year, the more evidence is gathered that the control has been effective.

Roll-forward testing is carried out at the year-end to provide management assurance over the internal control's effectiveness from the date that interim testing was carried out to the year-end, to complete the coverage over the whole period. The extent of roll-forward required should take into account the date of testing of the sample (and therefore the length of the remaining period to the year-end) and the possibility that there might be significant changes to internal control after the testing date.

TIP: In some circumstances, where a low risk has been identified that the control is no longer effective during the roll-forward procedure, inquiry alone may be sufficient as a roll-forward procedure. Otherwise, some form of roll-forward detailed testing will be required.

Where a control or controls have changed during the year, consideration must be given to whether testing must be carried out across the old and new controls, or whether the new controls supersede the old control.

The Audit Standard AS2201 allows the following as techniques for performing detailed testing:

- Inquiry of personnel (On its own, this technique is not sufficient testing to assess control effectiveness.)
- Observation of personnel;
- Observation of company's operations;
- Inspection of relevant documentation; and
- Re-performance of the control. (This technique gives the strongest evidence that the control was effective).

Evidence required to be documented to support the testing performed depends on the risk associated with the control.

The nature and extent of the testing of the internal control should take into the following risk factors:

- The nature of MMR that control is preventing or detecting;
- The inherent risk of financial account(s) and assertion(s);
- Any changes to the volume and nature of transactions during the period under review which may affect the operational effectiveness of the control;
- Whether the financial account has history of errors;
- The effectiveness of entity-level controls – especially controls which monitor the effective operation of other controls;
- The nature of control and frequency of operation;
- The degree to which control relies on effectiveness of other controls (e.g. IT General Controls);

- The competence of personnel (consider whether there have been any changes to personnel during the period and the arrangements in place for providing cover due to holidays or sickness absence);
- Segregation of duties between personnel performing the task or control and those with review or oversight responsibilities;
- Whether the control is manual or automated; and
- The complexity of the control and judgements which must be made in its operation.

Sample size

Controls are usually tested on a sample basis. The sample size is generally dependent on the frequency that the control is carried out i.e. half-yearly, monthly, weekly, daily, and continuously (or many times intra-day). The sample sizes are usually based on statistical sampling to provide a degree of underlying assurance and confidence in the full population of controls. Whilst beyond the scope of this book, sample sizes are based on the size of the population of controls to be tested, the confidence level to be achieved and the confidence interval.

TIP: There is good online guidance on reasonable sample sizes to be used for control testing from the AICPA website and from the 'Big 4' accountancy firms websites also. The standard AS2315 – Audit Sampling available on the PCAOB's website gives definitive guidance on sample sizes (refer to the section in the standard on Sampling in Tests of Controls) for external auditors and should also be followed by Management in its SOX 404 compliance testing.

TIP: We have seen previously that it is the aim of management testing of internal controls to arrive at the same conclusions and disclosures as the external auditors. It therefore makes sense to align sample testing sizes used by Management with the external auditors (who should normally be able to disclose the sample sizes they use). If Management uses the same sample sizes as the external auditors, this may also mean that they can inspect and may even potentially be able to rely on management testing for their purposes (where they deem it to be appropriate) thus making the external audit more efficient (and may drive down audit fees!) Any external auditor reliance on management testing would be at the auditor's discretion however.

6.5 TESTING WORKPAPERS AND SOX SOFTWARE

The SOX legislation requires that Management must keep all SOX 404 compliance testing workpapers for at least 7 years (this applies to both electronic and paper records). The SOX 404 compliance documentation should include the following:

- Planning: All planning documentation accumulated during the planning process and documentation of all decisions and conclusions reached ultimately leading to the annual plan of work.

- Walkthroughs: As previously described, walkthroughs must document the business process under review which should include: business process steps, internal controls, IT systems used, employees involved and locations; and the trial balance accounts or financial statement (including assertions) driven by transactions flowing through the process.

- Detailed testing documentation: Individual testing workpapers should identify the internal control being tested, the testing objectives (including linkages to the account assertions where appropriate), the audit work performed to test the control and the conclusions reached.

- The overall conclusions of the testing work performed should be fully documented including the impact of any control deficiencies identified on the overall conclusions reached. (This is covered in the next section).

All working papers should identify the person who carried out the work and the date it was carried out. Working papers should be subject to review by another (usually more senior) member of staff and would identify any review comments and follow up work carried out. Some auditors and company management delete review comments and earlier drafts of work papers once the reviewer has been satisfied that all review comments have been adequately followed up – in this case only the final version of the work paper is stored.

There are a number of SOX software packages on the market which facilitate documentation of the planning, walkthrough and detailed testing processes. These packages normally facilitate the SOX 404 compliance process including documentation of planning activities, selection of in-scope trial balance accounts and account assertions, linkage of in-scope accounts to walkthroughs and business process documentation and controls, control testing workpapers with conclusions reached, and assessment of deficiencies and the overall conclusions of work performed. Some SOX compliance packages automatically link to COSO and COBIT objectives (defined elsewhere) whereas others package are little more than working paper storage systems.

TIP: SOX software compliance testing packages will contain confidential information and so should have appropriate access restrictions to the SOX software. The work papers and data collected during the SOX compliance process should be subject to appropriate backup procedures to ensure they would be available for inspection for at least seven years.

6.6 TESTING CONCLUSIONS AND REPORTING

In order to summarize the conclusions of the SOX 404 compliance testing work, it is necessary to assess the impact both individually and collectively of all of the internal control deficiencies identified during the control testing process, to assess the risk that the internal control framework in place might not prevent a material misstatement from occurring.

The assessment process must consider whether one or more significant deficiencies or material weaknesses in the internal control framework have been identified. The PCAOB audit standard AU Section 325 "Communications About Control Deficiencies in an Audit of Financial Statements" provides helpful guidance and definitions.

Significant deficiencies

A *significant deficiency* is defined as "a deficiency, or a combination of deficiencies, in internal control over financial reporting, that is less severe than a material weakness yet important enough to merit attention by those responsible for oversight of the company's financial reporting."

It would be unusual for an individual internal control deficiency by itself to constitute a significant deficiency. Normally, in a company's internal control framework, there would be other compensating controls at business process level and also possibly at entity-level which would compensate for the control deficiency. A significant deficiency often occurs when there are several controls in the same business process which are not deficient, or perhaps a combination of business process and entity-level controls which are deficient in the same business area.

If oversight of internal and external financial reporting is ineffective, the circumstances should be categorized as at least a significant deficiency, and may suggest a possible material weakness in internal control over financial reporting.

If the external auditor determines that the oversight performed by the Audit Committee is ineffective, this must be communicated with a specific significant deficiency or material weakness in writing to the whole Board of Directors.

Material weakness

A *material weakness* is a deficiency, or a combination of deficiencies, in internal control over financial reporting, such that there is a reasonable possibility that a material misstatement of the company's annual or interim financial statements will not be prevented or detected on a timely basis.

The Audit Standard requires that all significant deficiencies and material weaknesses are reported to the external auditor, Management and the Audit Committee.

Conclusions

An overall conclusion for Management's testing of the SOX 404 internal control framework would be documented at the very end of the process and given to Management and the Audit Committee. The conclusions, including any significant deficiencies and material weaknesses, would feed into the overall attestation which the CEO and CFO must give in relation to internal reporting under SOX 404.

Significant deficiencies or material weaknesses should be reported in real-time rather than at the end of the work. Decisions about whether an interim communication should be issued should be decided based on relative significance of noted matters and urgency of follow-up action required.

A wider report containing all internal control deficiencies (or perhaps a summary) may be provided to the Audit Committee, Management and the external auditor although there is no requirement to do so.

If a material change is made to either disclosure controls and procedures, or to internal control over financial reporting, in response to a significant deficiency or material weakness, the company must disclose the change and contemplate whether it is necessary to make the disclosure of the significant deficiency in order to place the change in context.

It is mandatory that all material weaknesses must be publicly disclosed. It is not mandatory to publicly disclose the detail or nature of significant deficiencies. However, if there are a combination of significant deficiencies which are determined to be a material weakness overall – management must publicly disclose the material weakness and the nature of the significant deficiencies.

6.7 WORKPAPER RETENTION

It is a requirement under SOX legislation that management retains all its compliance testing documentation which supports its attestations and conclusions under SOX s302 and s404 for at least 7 years. This includes all paper records and electronic records. This should include evidence of management review of working papers and any challenge and follow up of issues. Many organizations use electronic working paper management systems which allow corporations to document their overall SOX 404 compliance testing and show how individual testing contributes to the overall management opinion and attestation on the financial statements. External auditors have the same requirement for their working papers.

7 IT INTERNAL CONTROLS

Business processes these days in just about every company large or small are underpinned by IT systems. In fact some businesses are now completely driven by IT with very little human intervention. So identification and evaluation of relevant IT controls is critical to the overall SOX 404 compliance process.

7.1 COBIT FRAMEWORK

The professional organization formerly known as Information Systems and Control Association (ISACA), now known only by its acronym ISACA, has developed a framework – Control Objectives for Information and Related Technologies (COBIT) which has become the international standard for the assessment of IT controls generally and specifically for SOX 404 compliance purposes. More information on ISACA and the COBIT framework (currently version 5) can be found at www.isaca.org. As with the COSO framework which we saw earlier, the COBIT framework is designed to provide a framework for good governance over IT functions generally and so has a much wider scope and remit than for SOX 404 compliance. The framework can be used to identify IT governance risks and controls but care should be taken to focus on those controls which contribute to IT systems and processes that fall within the scope of

SOX 404 compliance objectives.

7.2 ASSESSMENT OF IT INTERNAL CONTROLS

The assessment of IT controls has been split into 3 sections:

- Entity level controls applicable to IT: These are the controls which Management has in place to ensure that the IT function has appropriate policies, standards and processes, monitoring and management controls, and is appropriately arranged to underpin the IT General and IT application controls.

- IT Application controls: These are the business process level controls which control the access, input, processing and output of data from individual IT application programs.

- IT General controls: These are the controls in place over the underlying IT network, servers, databases and operating systems which underpin the IT applications and the business processes.

As has been described previously the COSO framework, and COBIT framework specifically for IT, can be used to define control objectives for IT internal controls and can assist Management in identifying suitable controls to satisfy the objectives and potential control gaps.

Where a control is missing or has not been designed effectively to satisfy the control objective (design deficiency) or where a control is not operating effectively (operational deficiency), the same processes for remediation of deficiencies should be followed as for business process internal control deficiencies found – refer Chapter 5: section 5.4 Internal control deficiencies. Also, the assessment of deficiencies and their reporting feeds into the overall conclusions of the SOX 404 compliance testing process described at Chapter 6: section 6.7 Testing conclusions and reporting.

7.3 ENTITY LEVEL CONTROLS APPLICABLE TO IT

We have already considered entity level controls as part of the SOX 404 compliance planning process. There may be entity level controls which are relevant to the effective operation of the IT function, systems and processes and therefore may be relevant to SOX 404 compliance processes. COBIT provides a number of control objectives which can be useful in identifying the specific relevant IT entity level controls.

Relevant IT entity-level controls may include any of the following:

Policies and standards

As well as the company-wide policies and standards, IT may have specific policies and standards e.g. IT security policy, which are particularly relevant to the operation of IT (e.g. in relation to how administrative-level access is governed). An assessment of the effectiveness of the entity-level control environment in IT would include an assessment of:

- Are all relevant IT standards and policies in place?
- Are they up-to-date and current?
- Are they published and available to staff who need to refer to them?
- Are employees given appropriate awareness and training?
- Are employees aware of their specific accountabilities in relation to the policies and standards which is relevant to their particular role?
- Are accountabilities written into employees' role descriptions / contracts of employment?
- Are employees' accountabilities under the standards and policies enforced by Management including in evaluations and in disciplinary processes if necessary?

IT function structure and management

The IT function should be structured (as should all functions!) to ensure segregation of duties in relation to IT general controls (described later). In particular, segregation of duties should generally be maintained between IT development and testing staff (who would not have access to the live systems or data) and IT operations staff (who have high-level access to the operational systems and data but not to development areas).

Oversight and monitoring of IT employee activities by line management in IT is a particular area of focus, especially where IT managers may not have the technical skills of the employees who often have high-level or administrator level access to systems and data.

Monitoring controls

Monitoring controls in place within IT to monitor the correct functioning of the IT systems.

Risk management and assurance functions

Entity-level controls within IT may include an assessment of the effectiveness of any specific risk management functions and processes operating within IT and any specific IT assurance functions.

7.4 IT APPLICATION CONTROLS

IT application controls are a particular type of business process controls and would be identified during the walkthrough process and tested as part of detailed testing.

IT application controls have been split into the following categories which are then defined in more detail:

-    Access to the IT application and its specific functions;

- Controls over data input;
- Controls over data processing; and
- Controls over data output.

Access to the IT application and its specific functions

An important control which supports the control objectives of a business process underpinned by an IT application is user access control to the IT application itself. This is usually achieved by requiring a user account and password to access the system. Access controls can support the occurrence (validity) control objective and fraud risk control objective in relation to financial transactions and records. They would often be underpinned by IT security policy and standards (which is covered in Entity-level controls over IT).

> **TIP:** Are users assigned unique user accounts and forced to maintain strong passwords which they must keep private?

Access controls can be used to enforce controls beyond simply limiting access to the system. They can be used to enforce segregation of duties controls such that they limit users' access to only the particular functions within the application relevant to their roles, e.g. the inputter of a journal cannot also authorize the same journal. They can also be used to facilitate authorizer controls e.g. certain managers with authorizer rights can authorize employee expense claims within the system.

> **TIP:** Access controls which enforce segregation of duties and facilitate other controls such as authorization of transactions are only ever as good as the currency of the user access list and associated access rights. The focus of controls testing should be on the process and controls for maintenance of the user list and users' access rights. Given that in most organizations, the application access administrator is often a relatively junior role, focus should be on the maintenance

of the currency of user access lists and rights including the authorization process for creation and updating of user access rights and the process for removal of leavers (or staff who have moved roles internally).

Controls over data input

There are generally two ways in which data can get into an IT application: either by manual input by an employee, or by an electronic interface or transfer from a prior IT system upstream in the business process. Controls over data input will generally support occurrence (validity) and sometimes completeness controls objectives such that data input controls ensure accurate input of valid, accurate and complete groups of financial records and transactions. Data input controls can also limit the ability for fraud to occur and so may support the fraud control objective.

Manual data input controls

There are a variety of manual input controls which may be applicable depending on the IT application and its place in the business process. The following is a list of possible manual data input controls which may be in place (the list is not exhaustive):

Access controls: as described earlier in this section

Matching input control: The same record is input twice and if it matches then the record is accepted as it is likely to be accurate if the same data has been input twice. Usually any mismatched fields are highlighted to the inputter for review and correction. This control is stronger if the record is input by separate employees and matched which may then also support the fraud risk control objective.

Review and authorization release control: Sometimes transactions are input and held in a 'holding area' within the IT application and require review and authorization by a different, and often more senior, user before transactions are 'released' into the system. There should be evidence that the review goes back to the source documentation of the transactions and that possibly incorrect transactions are highlighted for follow up and evidence of correction.

Input validation controls: These will vary depending on the IT system and the type of data input but could include forcing data fields not to be submitted blank; only allowing numeric characters in a number field; only allowing positive entries (for example for invoice payments) and setting tolerances, for example, not allowing tax fields which are outside an acceptable range.

Review of input: This is a detective control that might involve a report being produced containing the data input over a period of time. This report would then need to be reviewed and potential errors identified and followed up for correction.

Automated data input controls

These controls would apply over an automated feed or interface of data from an earlier IT application in the process into another application. They support the occurrence (validity) and sometimes completeness control objectives. The following are a list of possible automated data input controls (this is not exhaustive):

Reconciliation control: Reconciliation of data transferred between an upstream IT application and a downstream IT application (in a business process). This often can take the form of a report of the data records output by the upstream application, and sometimes a control total, which is compared with a report from the downstream application showing the number of records received (and control total). Discrepancies would then need to be followed up and errors rectified for this to be a valid control. Depending on the reconciliation performed, this may support the occurrence (validity) and completeness control objectives.

Automated validation and rejected records follow up: This control is where there are validation rules built into the interface between the two systems such that if a data record fails the validation process it is not accepted by the downstream application and is output into a rejected records file and/or report. These reports must be reviewed and followed up to correct errors for this to be a valid control.

Review of interface logs: The interface creates an audit log file or report when it runs and this is then reviewed to ensure that all errors are identified and followed up.

Automated processing controls

This is a 'control' which, in summary, means that if an IT application has been properly designed to process data in a correct way and produce expected output then it will continue to do that (2+2 always = 4!)

To obtain assurance that this is the case, there are a number of ways this can be done and to some extent will depend on the type of application and how it has been developed:

Third-party developed applications: Corporations often buy-in third-party developed applications e.g. for financial systems or payroll. In this case, comfort can be taken from purchasing from reputable long established suppliers who often provide testimonials and references from existing clients. That would not preclude a company from testing the software prior to implementation, to satisfy itself that the software will perform as expected. SOX 404 compliance testing might focus on the testing the company carries out on software it has purchased prior to it going live. (This is covered in more detail in the IT General Controls section)

In addition, software corporations will regularly release patches, upgrades, and fixes to update the software and to rectify issues which customers have brought to their attention. The focus of testing from a SOX 404 perspective would examine the process for ensuring that software was kept up-to-date, and patches and fixes were applied. It would also consider the extent of testing which has been carried out prior to any patches and upgrades being applied to the live software and the authorization controls in place prior to any changes being made to the live applications and/or data. (These are covered in more depth in Change Controls within the section on IT General Controls later).

In-house developed applications: Corporations often develop IT applications in-house or will buy in a third-party developed software package and then significantly tailor it in-house to meet the company's specific needs.

From a SOX 404 compliance perspective, obtaining assurance that the IT application will process data correctly as expected will largely come from the controls which would have been in force during the stages of the application's development process. (This is covered off in much more depth in the Systems Development Lifecycle within the IT General Controls section and has not been repeated here).

TIP: A practical issue for SOX 404 compliance in this area is that often IT applications were developed some time, often years, in the past, and it's simply not practical or useful to examine the system development controls that were used to develop the system in the first place. In this case, sometimes it can be useful simply to re-perform some of the processing functions of the application (either manually or in other software e.g. Excel) if that is feasible, to prove that the system works as expected it may also be appropriate to examine the entity-level monitoring controls that might be in place to detect that an IT application has stopped processing as expected and therefore produces unexpected output, would be detected and fixed.

As for third-party developed applications, there will be an ongoing process to implement updates and fixes to in-house developed software. SOX 404 compliance testing would focus on the controls over this process including the adequacy of testing and authorization of changes made to the live application. (These are covered in more depth in Change Controls within the section on IT General Controls later).

Data output controls

Data output controls the opposite side of the data input controls highlighted above and would apply where, having been processed in some way, data is output from a system either onto a report for follow up or to go into a downstream system for further processing. The following are examples of some data output controls (list not exhaustive):

Reconciliation of data: Reconciliation of data between the upstream application and the downstream application. This often can take the form of a report of the data records output by the upstream application and often a control total, which is then compared with a report from the downstream application showing the number of records received and control total. Discrepancies between the two reports would then need to be followed up and errors rectified for this to be a valid control. Depending on the reconciliation performed, this may support the occurrence (validity) and completeness control objectives.

Review of output: This is a detective control that would involve a report being produced containing the data output over a period of time. This report would then need to be reviewed and potential errors identified and followed up for correction for this to be a valid control.

7.5 IT GENERAL CONTROLS

In the previous section, we have looked at the controls over the flows of data and financial transactions between individual IT applications. However, these applications sit on an IT infrastructure which may include: servers, IT networks, databases, and connections to the outside world and the Internet. Therefore the effectiveness, or otherwise, of IT controls can be strengthened, or indeed undermined, by the strength of the underlying IT controls operating over the IT infrastructure. These controls are called IT General Controls and have been split into the following categories:

- IT Access Controls
- IT System Development Lifecycle Controls
- IT Change Control
- IT Backup and Disaster Recovery Controls
- IT Operational Controls

IT Access controls

As described previously, IT access controls should be underpinned by IT security policy and standards. There should be appropriate controls over access to the components of the IT infrastructure. Whilst the detail of the access restrictions and controls that might be required is a specialist area which is well beyond the scope of this book, however some key general questions are listed below which should address the main points (list not exhaustive):

IT servers: If users can gain access to IT servers' operating systems, they can often have the ability to inadvertently, or deliberately, alter IT software or data directly (financial transaction data, user access logs) – bypassing IT application controls. Therefore, for SOX 404 compliance, it is relevant to consider the effectiveness of access controls that are in place over the IT servers' operating systems such that they are appropriately restricted, managed, logged and monitored. The effectiveness of the use of the 'administrator' or similar user account should be considered. Also, IT operating systems can often be configured to varying degrees of 'lockdown' which prevents unauthorized access, and it can be relevant to consider the degree of configuration and 'lockdown' which has been applied to the IT servers' operating systems.

Databases: Databases are used to store the underlying financial transactions, as well as other data such as supplier and customer data. Therefore it is relevant for SOX 404 compliance purposes, in relation to the integrity of the financial transactions, and to prevent fraud, that access to the underlying databases is appropriately secured and 'locked down'; controls are in place over underlying or administrator access, and that all access and changes made to underlying data is appropriately logged and monitored.

IT networks and other infrastructure: This is well beyond the scope of this book, however to support the integrity of financial transactions and to prevent fraud, both of which are SOX 404 compliance objectives, it may be necessary to examine the controls over the operation of IT networks and other IT infrastructure. This could include the controls over monitoring of unauthorized access, both internally and externally, to IT networks; controls over configuration and access to firewalls which restrict access to IT networks from the Internet and the outside world; and controls over configuration of the IT network itself. It may also be relevant to consider how the connection of an unauthorized device to a company's IT network would be prevented and/or detected, and the extent to which virus controls are in place. It may also be relevant to consider how IT controls might prevent or detect users from running unauthorized software – either via email, from flash drives or from CDs.

IT System Development Lifecycle Controls

Some larger organizations (and increasingly in the Internet era – smaller organizations) are going down the route of developing their own IT application internally to support their businesses. As was mentioned earlier in the IT application controls section, the correct processing of data is relevant for SOX 404 compliance, and for in-house developed applications, is dependent on controls which have operated during the development of the system, which are often described as IT System Development Lifecycle controls. A full description of the System Development Lifecycle is beyond the scope of this book; however some of the key areas of focus are summarized below:

IT system specification and design: The specification and design is sufficiently detailed and documented by stakeholders.

Unit testing: There has been sufficient testing of individual units of code to ensure that errors are detected and corrected.

Integration testing: Testing is performed on the software application as a whole and that testing is sufficiently comprehensive. This would include testing the software functionality in all different respects, using different data sets, which would be representative of the data which would be expected in live operation. Again there should be evidence that all errors have been followed up and corrected.

User acceptance testing: Users' representatives test the application in sufficient depth to be able to test the functionality as set out in the original system specification and design to ensure that the application performs as expected. Again all errors found should be followed up and corrected.

TIP: Testing would normally not be performed in the live IT environment, but in a separate test IT environment. Consideration should be given to how closely the test environment mirrors the live environment, particularly the extent to which the test environment replicates the integration of the application under development with other internal IT applications and external connections to third-parties and the Internet. (Differences between the test and live IT environment can mean that errors and discrepancies are not identified during testing which may then surface during live processing).

To help ensure that the IT application operates in the live environment as expected, it is important the testing environment replicates as closely as possible, the live environment, and therefore the data that is used for testing should mirror, as closely as possible, the data which the application would be expected to process in real life (including all the richness and complexity of data combinations which might exist). If the data already exists, then consideration should be given to using live datasets (running in the test environment - of course) and ensuring that the data sets used for testing would give sufficient assurance over all the possible scenarios (e.g. for financial systems that could include period end processing as well as normal day-to-day processing).

It is often difficult, or impractical, to test the IT system development controls which occurred in the past (and sometimes in the distant past) over the development of the live IT applications in use today. SOX 404 compliance testing programs may test the current controls over IT applications in development to provide assurance in the future when the application goes live. For live IT applications in use today, which may not have been subjected to SOX 404 testing at the time of their development, it may be appropriate to identify other ways of providing assurance over the correct operation and processing of those systems.

Controls over promotion to live: There are review and authorization controls which are in place to ensure that all testing has been carried out as planned (and if not, why not, and what the consequences of any limitation of testing might be). In addition, all defects and errors found during testing have been rectified, and if some errors had not been fixed, perhaps because they had been deemed to be too small in impact but difficult to rectify, what the overall impacts of these unrectified defects would be individually, and in combination.

Live monitoring: As described later in the section on IT Operational Controls, there would be monitoring controls in place which monitor the correct operation of IT systems. Monitoring processes and controls may be enhanced and closer monitoring might be carried out in the immediate aftermath of a change have been made to ensure it has not caused an unexpected error or discrepancy in the IT application's processing or data.

IT Change Control

Changes are often required to live IT applications. Changes can be required due to errors found by users; software updates or upgrades from suppliers e.g. updated tax rates in payroll systems; and changes as a result of changes of requirements by users e.g. new reports. This applies whether software has been developed in-house or by a third-party software developer.

Therefore to ensure the correct functionality and processing of data by IT applications, the effectiveness of IT change controls in place can be relevant for SOX 404 compliance purposes.

Assessment of the effectiveness of IT change control usually involves consideration of the individual stages in the change control process:

Testing: Changes or updates to software should be thoroughly tested in a test IT environment prior to being made live. Assessment of the effectiveness of the testing process, as has been described previously in relation to testing controls, would consider: the extent to which the test environment mirrors the live IT environment (and therefore the extent to which the results in test would replicate the results of live processing); the extent of testing of different functionality and reporting as a result of the change; and the extent of testing using different data sets. As with all testing, it is only effective if errors are identified, followed up and subsequently corrected. Testing would identify the expected result, the actual result, whether the test was a 'pass' or 'fail' – if a 'fail' what the corrective action was; and would include sign-off and date by the tester and reviewer.

Authorization of changes: Changes to live programs and data should be authorized by an appropriate individual prior to being made live, and the authorization process would consider the purpose of the change; the potential impacts of the change (and perhaps an overall risk assessment); the extent of testing performed and the results of that testing. On occasion, there may be a requirement to make emergency changes to live applications or data due to a business critical issue. In these (hopefully rare) occasions, consideration should be given to the extent to which testing is performed retrospectively on changes to confirm that there are no adverse results from the change; the extent to which the live running of the application is monitored for any unexpected results after the change (see below); and the ability to back-out and revert to a stable state prior to the change should be considered.

Monitoring of live running: The monitoring of live running of applications in general is covered within IT Operational controls below, however the monitoring of the correct processing of applications may be intensified in the period after a change (particularly in respect of an emergency change) to ensure that there are no unexpected processing results or data caused by the change.

Promotion to live: This is a process and control by which a change to a program or data is 'promoted' or implemented in the live environment. This process is normally carried out by an IT administrator who has confirmed that the appropriate authorization is in place.

Back-out process: If a change has been made to an IT application or data which is subsequently found to be in error, then there should be a process in place to allow safe back-out of the change and to revert to a known stable state prior to the change being implemented. This may be important for SOX 404 compliance purposes particularly if financial data or the processing of data is the subject of the change.

IT Backup and Disaster Recovery controls

Corporations take backups of their software and data which allows them to recover their IT systems in the event of a problem or a disaster with the live IT systems. Backups can be incremental (i.e. the backup might only be capturing the changes to programs and/or data since the previous backup) or it might be a total image taken of the full system. Increasingly the cloud is being used to store data and run programs which may change the requirement for corporations to make their own backups of programs and data. (Consideration of the controls at processes run by third parties are covered in chapter 8 – Outsourced processes and controls).

Consideration of the effectiveness of the IT backup and disaster recovery controls would include assessment of the schedule and type of backups taken; the storage of those backups and the extent to which testing has been performed on backups to prove that they are able to restore the system to a current (or recent) state without introducing new errors caused by the backup process.

IT Operational Controls

IT departments operate a number of operational controls and processes which monitor the correct operation and processing of the IT applications and data. These may include operational batch processing results reports; error reports; and real-time flagging of issues. Many IT departments operate 'dashboards' which give real-time status monitoring of applications and data and allow IT departments to react quickly to errors detected.

8 OUTSOURCED PROCESSES AND CONTROLS

Many corporations choose to outsource specific business functions and processes to be run by other organizations. These can include operational functions such as call centers, IT functions and finance functions. Many of these outsourced business processes can be involved in initiating or processing financial transactions (or could be at risk of fraud) and so can be in scope when considering SOX 404 compliance.

For SOX 404 compliance purposes, outsourced processes and controls must be considered as if they were running and operating within the company itself. However, it would normally be very impractical for corporations to send auditors to their outsourced business process providers. Most outsourced business process providers have a number of clients and so would grind to a halt if all of their clients sent auditors to fulfil their SOX 404 compliance requirements. In order to avoid the need for this, outsourced business process providers often engage their external auditors to perform compliance audit work over their business processes and controls.

This work is done following the Statement on Standards for Attestation Engagements no. 16 (SSAE 16) – Reporting on Controls at a Service Organization. The report produced is called a Service

Organization Controls 1 (SOC 1) report.

A SOC 1 report focuses on controls at the service organization that would be useful to corporations and their auditors for the purpose of planning a financial statement audit of the user entity and evaluating internal control over financial reporting at the company. The SOC 1 report contains the service organization's system description and an assertion from management. In addition, the independent service organization's external auditor (i.e., CPA firm) opinion or service auditor report is included.

There are two types of SOC 1 report: Type 1 and Type 2.

Type 1: This report covers the system's description and operation at a specific point in time. In a Type I report, the service auditor expresses an opinion and report on the subject matter provided by the management of the service organization as to (1) whether the service organization's description of its system fairly presents the service organization's system that was designed and implemented as of a specific date; and (2) whether the controls related to the control objectives stated in management's description of the service organization's system were suitably designed to achieve those control objectives - also as at a specified date.

Type 2: This report covers the service operation system's description and detailed testing of the key internal controls in place over a period of time – normally over a period of at least six months. In a Type II report, the service auditor expresses an opinion and report on the subject matter provided by the management of the service organization as to (1) whether the service organization's description of its system fairly presents the service organization's system that was designed and implemented throughout the specified period; (2) whether the controls related to the control objectives stated in management's description of the service organization's system were suitably designed throughout the specified period to achieve those control objectives; and (3) whether the controls related to the control objectives stated in management's description of the service organization's system operated effectively throughout the specified period to achieve those control objectives.

SOC 2 and SOC 3 reports are designed to allow service organizations to give information about their system description in accordance with specific criteria related to availability, security, and confidentiality.

> **TIP**: SOC 2 and SOC 3 type reports are not necessarily relevant for SOX 404 compliance objectives, but they may provide useful information e.g. in relation to IT general controls over access.
>
> The SOC 1 report Type 1, because it assesses the service organization's system and internal controls at a specific point in time is not generally useful for providing SOX 404 compliance.
>
> A service provider's SOC 1 report Type II will provide sufficient assurance for SOX 404 compliance purposes for both company's management and for its external auditors. It is important to ensure that the scope of the work performed under SSAE16 covers the outsourced processes which the service organization performs along with relevant IT, Finance and back office processes which may be in-scope for a company's SOX 404 compliance purposes. In addition, corporations need to ensure that service organizations provide SOC 1 reports covering the system and testing of internal controls for the full period required for SOX 404 compliance. On occasion, the SOC 1 report's end date may be earlier than the company's annual report date. In these cases, the service organization's auditor may be required to provide a bridging letter providing assurance for SOX 404 compliance purposes from the end date of the SOC 1 report to the company's annual report date.
>
> If a SOC 1 report is being produced to the same date as the annual report, on a practical level, corporations should hold discussions with their service providers to ensure that SOC 1 reports are received in good time for their incorporation to the overall SOX 404 compliance

assessment of internal control.

All control deficiencies identified in the service organization's SOC 1 report should be treated, assessed and reported on as if they were control deficiencies in the company's own framework of internal controls – refer to the section on Control Deficiencies for more detail.

TIP: Corporations will normally have Key Performance Indicators (KPIs) and other operational measures built into the contracts they have with service organizations. The monitoring of KPIs and other performance measures by management is a good entity-level control for SOX 404 compliance purposes.

9 CERTIFICATION FRAMEWORKS

The CEO and CFO may request sub certifications as part of the overall SOX 404 compliance framework to receive certifications from managers that internal control structures and financial reporting procedures have operated correctly during the period being certified. However, the SOX legislation and the SEC have made it clear that the CEO and CFO are still accountable under SOX, and this accountability for the operation and effectiveness of internal controls ultimately still lies with the CEO and CFO and cannot be delegated. It is a useful exercise to run sub certifications however which puts management and employees on notice as to what the company's expectations are of them in relation to SOX: specifically in relation to the operation of internal controls and for identification and escalation of financial errors and misstatements. It increases the likelihood that internal controls are operated and policies and procedures have been complied with during the period. It also gives another route for line management to escalate issues (albeit any issues should have already been called out through existing risk management framework and management processes). Certification processes may also call out control issues not identified through the SOX 404 compliance testing which is carried out on a sample basis.

TIP: If a sub certification process is to be run, then consideration should be given to providing guidance and training on the expectations for the certification process to those managers who are going to receive the certification for the first time (and also for new managers who join the company at a later date).

It is useful to have in place a sub certification process operating quarterly at period ends which helps support the management certifications required by s302 of SOX for quarterly financial reporting to the market (and can roll-up to the annual SOX s404 annual internal controls evaluation and annual report certifications.)

If a sub certification process is put in place, some typical recipients would be:
- Company Executives.
- Departmental controllers.
- Vice Presidents.
- Risk management function managers or other assurance function employees.
- IT managers.
- Finance function managers.

Consideration should be given to how far down the corporate management structure the certification process should go. Operational staff may feel that signing a certification like this is a level of responsibility that goes beyond their role description or contract of employment. There should be a consistent level of application of the certification process across the business (i.e. if certain grades of middle or lower management are included or excluded from the certification process – this should generally be consistent in different functions of the business, or it should be made clear why not if not).

Certifications would normally cover the following areas:

- The period under certification.
- The function or department which the manager certifying is responsible for (and possibly also locations if that is relevant).
- The responsibilities of the manager in relation to the effective operation of internal controls.
- Relevant policies and procedures (including ethics policies and codes of conduct) have been understood and complied with during the period.
- Management certification that the internal controls and financial reporting processes under their responsibility have been operating effectively throughout the period. Sometimes the certification will specifically identify and list the individual internal controls required for SOX 404 compliance and ask for those to be certified.
- There is usually space for management to formally document any issues which may have prevented the internal controls from operating effectively during the period and/or where a significant financial reporting error may have occurred during the period which may not have been corrected. (Definitions and/or context may have to be provided to management here as to what would be relevant to document here).
- A statement of the expectations and/or manager's accountability for the integrity and completeness of the information provided (and perhaps sometimes the consequences and likely sanctions if incorrect or incomplete information is provided).
- The time limit for providing a response.
- What happens if the manager who should provide the certification is absent e.g. off sick or on holiday?

TIP: The sub certification process is often run either by the SOX compliance team (if such a team exists within the company) or sometimes the Risk or Finance function. The certification process should be reviewed and updated each time it is run to ensure that a) all corporate changes to the structure of the company and locations are reflected in the certifications to ensure that the certifications cover all relevant functions and locations and b) that managers have been updated to the current post holders.

Consideration should be given to how changes in management during the period under certification are handled to ensure certification is obtained that covers the full period of the certification (i.e. whether the new manager is expected to still certify the whole period under review – they might require specific guidance on how to achieve that). Sometimes the line manager of the outgoing manager must provide the certification for the earlier period and the new manager only provides certification for period covering their tenure.

It is sometimes helpful to ask second line assurance functions to provide certifications. As second line functions, they should have no direct responsibility for the operation of internal controls, however it is useful to provide comfort over the operation of entity level controls that second line managers are asked to provide certification that a) their functions operated effectively during the period and that b) all issues affecting SOX relevant internal controls (including potential financial misstatement and fraud) and/or misstatements in financial reporting which may have gone uncorrected have been all reported and escalated. This may require a certification which is more specifically tailored to second line function processes and responsibilities.

Management sub certification processes are not required in order for a company's management to provide an evaluation of its internal controls and financial reporting processes under s404 of SOX, however it is a useful additional process which makes clear expectations of management and employees, and increases the likelihood of compliance with policies, procedures and effective internal controls. It also gives management another route to call out issues affecting internal controls and financial reporting errors. However, it should not be used as a tool for line management to absolve themselves of responsibility for the proper functioning of the internal controls in their business functions. It should be noted that however many certification processes are put in place, they do not absolve the CEO and CFO of their accountability for the certifications they must make under s.302 and s.404 of SOX (and the penalties they face for getting those wrong!)

10 OTHER REFORMS INTRODUCED BY SOX

There were other reforms introduced by the SOX Act which helped strengthen the corporate governance framework.

10.1 AUDIT COMMITTEE

The SOX Act requires that corporations must establish an Audit Committee. The Audit Committee must be comprised of Directors of the Board and must be independent of management. They must only receive payment from the company for the role they play in being Directors and cannot receive remuneration for any other work e.g. consultancy. They also cannot be affiliated with the company through family relationships or employment ties. The Committee receives the output of management's testing of Internal Controls which is required by SOX 404 (see the relevant section for more details on SOX 404 testing). The Committee is also responsible for overseeing the work of the external auditor and receives their audit report. The Audit Committee has the authority to engage outside experts, advisors, and auditors which the company must pay for if required.

The CEO, and the CFO (and other executives from time-to-time) will attend Audit Committee meetings, but they are not members of the Audit Committee, cannot vote and the Audit Committee is expected to meet at times in closed session without any executives present.

> **TIP:** One person on the Audit Committee must be a financial expert or, if there are no financial experts, then the Audit Committee must hire in external expertise sufficient to provide the relevant financial expertise.
>
> The Audit Committee must establish procedures for handling "accounting, internal accounting controls or auditing matters" including "confidential, anonymous submission by employees...of concerns regarding questionable accounting or auditing matters".
>
> The statement above refers to whistleblowing procedures which must be established under SOX. The Audit Committee must be the recipient of all whistleblowing tip offs and must be empowered to take appropriate action as it sees fit depending on the nature of the tip off received.

10.2 UPDATES TO FILINGS WITH THE SEC

This section focuses on the main reports which are filed by publicly listed corporations with the SEC and the main changes to those brought about by SOX (It is not a comprehensive list of all filings with the SEC!)

There are three main reports filed with the SEC that changed as a result of the SOX legislation:

10-K   This is the annual filing made by all listed corporations with the SEC that contains the company's annual report and financial statements.

The SOX Act requires that the annual report must contain a certification by the CEO and CFO as described in more detail elsewhere in the guide. The annual report must also contain an

Internal Controls report stating that management is responsible for the internal control structure and procedures for financial reporting and that management has assessed the effectiveness of the internal controls for the previous year. It also must document the results of that assessment.

SOX requirements mean that the financial statements filed with the 10-K must reflect material corrections and adjustments to the financial statements made by the external auditors to the draft financial statements. They must also include details of all material off-balance sheet transactions and relationships. The 10-K must also include details of changes in securities ownership by Management, Directors, and principal stockholders. It should also contain formation on whether these individuals have adopted a code of ethics.

10-Q   This is the quarterly financial update that is made by all listed corporations to update the market and investors on the progress by the company on its financial targets since the publication of the annual report. The 10-Q must be certified by the CEO and CFO under s302 of SOX. It usually contains less information than the annual report and does not contain a SOX 404 certification on internal controls.

8-K This is a 'real-time' report to the SEC which is required when an applicable event, which requires to be reported, has occurred – usually with four working days of the event occurring.

There are a number of events that must be disclosed on an 8-K:

- Entry into, or termination of, a material agreement.
- Creation of a new material obligation.
- Defaulting on a financial obligation or moving up the date when the obligation is due.
- Ceasing a commercial activity.
- Write-offs.

- Failure to meet stock exchange reporting requirements.
- Restating previously issued financial statements.
- Departing directors and officers.

The SOX Act required some new events to be disclosed on an 8-K to the market (and also moved some events from being disclosed at the next quarter to real-time disclosure):

- Significant sales- sales of more than 1% of outstanding or new shares.
- Changes in rights of shareholders.
- Amendments to the company's bylaws and articles.
- Bankruptcy or receivership.
- Purchase of significant financial assets.
- Changes in auditors.
- Changes in financial control policies.
- Suspension of employee rights to transfer 401K (pension plan).
- Changes in, or waivers of, ethics policies for financial officers.

If a company fails to report an event on an 8-K then the SEC will suspend taking significant action if the event is reported to the market on the next 10-Q (with the exception of material omissions or misstatements in the financial statements). However, if a company fails to report an 8-K on time then it will be subject to SEC penalties and the SEC may treat the company as being more risky from a governance perspective, and subject it to a more rigorous oversight regime. Investors and the market will also take a very dim view of management if a company fails to meet its market reporting obligations on time.

Filings

These company filings (and many others) are filed with the SEC online using its EDGAR system. EDGAR stands for Electronic Data Gathering, Analysis and Retrieval system. EDGAR performs automated collection, validation, indexing, acceptance and forwarding of submissions by corporations to the SEC. It increases efficiency and transparency by accelerating the dissemination and analysis of corporate information to investors, the market and the public. Some documents may not be submitted electronically to EDGAR and must be filed manually with the SEC.

Corporate documents filed with EDGAR can be viewed online at www.sec.gov. The website has an easy to use search facility which can identify the corporation and the document required.

11 WHISTLEBLOWING

The SOX legislation introduced a number of protections for whistleblowers. Under section 806 of SOX, an employee is engaging in protected whistleblower conduct by providing information that they reasonably believe is a violation of:

- federal mail, wire, bank, or securities fraud;
- federal law relating to fraud against shareholders;
- any rule or regulation of the Securities and Exchange Commission (SEC).

SOX section 806 forbids any officers, employees, contractors, sub-contractors and agents of the company from retaliating against a whistleblower. If there is alleged retaliation against a whistleblower then the legislation gives whistleblowers the right to sue the company and its employees for reinstatement and back pay.

There are a number of other provisions within the SOX Act that relate to whistleblowers.

We have already looked at the SOX requirement for creation of Audit Committees. As part of the Audit Committee function, corporations must establish procedures to enable employees to file internal whistleblower complaints. These procedures must also protect the confidentiality of employees who file allegations with the Audit Committee.

The SOX Act, and the SEC's implementing regulations, require lawyers, under certain circumstances, to blow the whistle on their employer or client, thereby removing protection of client privilege, if they suspect wrongdoing in relation to section 806 as outlined earlier in this chapter.

SOX also amended the federal obstruction of justice statute and criminalized retaliation against whistleblowers. This is applicable to all employers in the United States, not only publicly traded corporations.

Lastly, Section 3(b) of the SOX Act contains an enforcement provision concerning every clause of the Act. This section grants jurisdiction to the SEC to enforce every aspect of the SOX Act, including the various whistleblower-related provisions. It also provides for criminal penalties for any violation of the SOX, including the whistleblower-related provisions.

As mentioned earlier in the book, the whistleblowing provisions provided by the SOX Act were extended in 2010 by the Dodd-Frank Act in the following ways:

- It created a compulsory bounty program by which whistleblowers can receive between 10% to 30% of the proceeds recovered from a litigation settlement.

- It broadened the scope of employees covered by the legislation by including employees of the company as well as its subsidiaries and affiliates.

- It extended the statute of limitations under which a whistleblower can bring forward a claim against his employer from 90 to 180 days after a violation is discovered.

The Dodd-Frank Act also brought into being the SEC's Office of the Whistleblower which oversees the SEC's whistleblower program.

12 UPDATE FEBRUARY 2018

The most significant change to the SOX framework since this book was originally written in November 2016 has been the introduction by the PCAOB in June 2017 of a new audit standard AS3101: " The Auditor's Report on an Audit of Financial Statements When the Auditor Expresses an Unqualified Opinion" and related amendments to other auditing standards. This snappily titled audit standard came into force for audits of fiscal year ends on or after 15 December 2017.

This standard now requires the communication of Critical Audit Matters (CAMs) for many audits conducted under PCAOB standards. (There a few classes of corporations, e.g. brokers and dealers operating under the SEC Act 1934 Rule 17a-5, to which CAM communication does not apply, however the audit standard should be referred to for specific details of exclusions.)

Critical Audit Matters

CAMs are any matters arising from the audit of the financial statements communicated, or required to be communicated, to the audit committee and that (1) relate to accounts or disclosures that are material to the financial statements; and (2) involved especially challenging, subjective, or complex auditor judgment.

In determining CAMs, the auditor will be required to take into account specific factors such as the auditor's risk assessment, areas in the financial statements that involved the application of significant judgment or estimation by management, significant unusual transactions, and the nature and extent of audit effort and evidence necessary to address the matter.

The auditor's report will be required to (1) identify the CAM; (2) describe the principal considerations that led the auditor to determine the matter is a CAM; (3) describe how it was addressed in the audit; and (4) make reference to the relevant financial statement accounts and disclosures. If the auditor determines there are no CAM, the auditor must state so in the auditor's report.

The provisions relating to CAM will take effect for audits for fiscal years ending on or after June 30 2019 for large accelerated filers; and for fiscal years ending on or after December 15 2020 for all other corporations to which the requirements apply.

The other significant change introduced by AS3101 is that the auditor's report will be required to include a statement disclosing the year in which the auditor began serving consecutively as the company's auditor ("auditor tenure"). A number of other changes to existing requirements are intended to clarify the auditor's role and responsibilities and make the auditor's report easier to read. These requirements include (1) addressing the auditor's report to the company's shareholders and the board of directors; (2) standardizing the form of the auditor's report; (3) disclosing that the auditor is required to be independent; and (4) adding the phrase "whether due to error or fraud," when describing the auditor's responsibilities under PCAOB standards to obtain reasonable assurance about whether the financial statements are free of material misstatement.

13 REFERENCE MATERIALS

There are a large number of reference materials in relation to the SOX Act (and previous and subsequent legislation) and in relation to the SOX certification and compliance process.

As has been said in the disclaimer at the beginning of this guide, this book has not been designed to be a comprehensive reference manual to all aspects of SOX, but gives the reader a summary of the main components of SOX and a practical guide to building and maintaining a SOX compliance program.

If you are looking for further information and guidance, there are a number of websites which contain information on various aspects of the legislation, current news, audit standards, resource material and forums where intelligence can be shared and questions can be asked.

Wikipedia – The online encyclopedia has a large number of pages devoted to all aspects of the SOX legislation and related audit standards.

PCAOB – The PCAOB (www.pcaobus.org) website contains lots of resources and in particular is useful for getting the up-to-date audit standards.

SEC – The SEC website (www.sec.gov) contains lots of useful information relevant to listed corporations and users can browse the filings of all registered corporations using the EDGAR system.

www.sox-online.com - This website has lots of links to SOX resources and information. It is user maintained so be wary of material being out-of-date.

COSO – The COSO website (www.coso.org) contains all of the relevant resources applicable to all aspects of the COSO ERM framework. **TIP:** Note that COSO charges for all of its resources and, depending on your organization, not all may be applicable, so try to ensure that you only buy the relevant resources for your needs.

ISACA – www.isaca.org The ISACA website contains all the relevant resources to ISACA itself, the CISA IT auditor qualification, and the COBIT IT controls framework.

TIP: ISACA charges for access to all of its COBIT resources to work out exactly which resources are relevant to your SOX 404 compliance needs before you purchase.

SSAE16 – www.ssae16.com   this website contains some useful information and resources on SSAE16 reports. It is user maintained though so be wary of information being out-of-date or obsolete.

TIP: There are also a number of decent reference books for SOX on the market (apart from this one obviously!) and they be a useful resource. It is worth checking out when they were last updated as a few have fallen quite out-of-date and looking at their reviews online before purchasing to find out what other purchasers thought of them.

Printed in Great Britain
by Amazon

79836114R00068